Phantom Limb

AMERICAN LIVES SERIES

Series Editor: Tobias Wolff

Phantom Limb

Janet Sternburg

UNIVERSITY OF NEBRASKA PRESS

Lincoln and London

© 2002 by Janet Sternburg
All rights reserved
Manufactured in the United
States of America
⊖ Library of Congress
Cataloging-in-Publication Data
Sternburg, Janet.
Phantom limb: a memoir /
Janet Sternburg.   p. cm. –
(American lives series)
ISBN 0-8032-4296-4 (cl.: alk.
paper) 1. Aging parents – Care
– United States. 2. Aging
parents – United States –
Psychology. 3. Aging parents –
United States – Family
relationships. 4. Adult children
of aging parents – United
States – Psychology. 5. Loss
(Psychology) 6. Bereavement
I. Title. II. Series. HQ1063.6 .S76
2002 305.26'0973 – dc21
2001045113

N,

for S. D. L.

Phantom Limb

1 The eternal mystery of oars
Plowing back as the boat floats forward,
So our deeds and words plow toward the past
For the body to go forward with the person
inside.

Yehuda Amichai from *The Eternal Mystery*

I open the bedroom door and come upon my mother as she is pulling an ivory cotton knit sweater over her head. Her bra, her panty hose, her skin, all are ivory. Around her head and completely enclosing it is a large mesh hood zipped down the middle of her face. Protected as a beekeeper, her features are barely perceptible. Her makeup will be intact. Lipstick will not smear nor powder dust her clothes. She is, for a second, immobile: a ghost surprised by her progeny.

She emerges 'nicely put together,' one of her favorite phrases. She's wearing her wig, ordered some years ago from a catalog. At this age it makes her look pinched. She takes pride in maintaining her possessions, faithfully placing the wig each night on a long-necked styrofoam head, something like a classical Roman bust but very light to carry.

Today she puts the head in a shopping bag and gives it to my father, who takes it downstairs on the elevator along with her over-night bag. In a few minutes the buzzer rings, signaling that he has brought the car around.

On the trip to the hospital, it is I who drives, silently rehearsing for an explosion that may come when my father notices I'm taking a route different from his own. My father is sitting beside me, my mother in the back, the three of us in a very different configuration from the way we sat on our weekly drive in our 1950s Buick with its mighty fins. Then I was in the middle, dying for air. My mother would be looking out at Boston's suburbs – Newton, Wellesley – charmed names of towns where she wished she lived. She'd point out a handsomely carved fence, an especially beautiful fanlight above a door painted colonial red.

'Those aren't houses for just anybody,' she'd say.

She'd also admire more modest one-family homes with pleasant yards, maybe an occasional magnolia with buds swollen to the size of eggs, or a doorstep on which a Halloween jack-o'-lantern could be placed; the kind of house her friends lived in, the ones who had married what in her eyes were successful men.

'I bet they're not as nice as our apartment,' I'd say, wanting to cushion my father from the rebuke implied in her envy.

'That's a beautiful color,' I'd say too, wanting to make my mother feel appreciated for her fine eye, even for the justice of her longing.

On good days, my father would turn to my mother and croon their song, 'I'm in love with you, Always, With a love that's true, Always . . .' She'd put her hand on his knee.

'Oh, Lou.'

My father would send my mother hugely oversized flowery valentines. Sometimes she'd stand behind him when he was sitting at dinner and lean over to kiss the top of his bald head. 'I love the smell of you,' she'd say, at those moments unlike herself much of the time, when headaches made her flinch from light and touch.

On other days, my father would spot an alluring side road and make a quick swerve, often in the face of a car coming toward us. I'd be thrilled at the prospect of seeing something new. My mother, though, would make a fearful little gasp.

'Lou, what are you doing?'

Behind us, the horn of a car sounded.

Over his shoulder, my father called, 'You jackass.'

'Sh-sh,' my mother said.

The angry driver had passed. 'You moron,' my father yelled.

My mother kept sh-shing him.

He shook off her hand.

'Don't sh-sh me. Stupid idiot . . .'

'Stop it!' my mother ordered, as though speaking to an errant dog.

His face got redder and redder.

'Get out. Both of you.'

I kept my hand on the door handle, in case. Only when I could see our own building did I let go. My mother loosened her thumb from inside her fist.

I drop them off at the main entrance to the hospital, waiting to see my father propel my mother safely through the revolving door before I spiral up the garage, its too-narrow turns requiring both hands on the wheel, a parking ticket clamped between my lips. I gather up the bag with my mother's nightgowns, her toiletries carefully packed in a clear plastic case, and head to the lobby.

As I wait for the elevator, I look around. Beside me are men and women in their forties and fifties, all carrying something: shopping bags, flowers. They look worried as I am, a weary congregation at this particular time in our lives.

The next day when I take the elevator to her floor, the door opens to a long corridor. My mother pads toward me in her velour slippers and mandarin-collared robe with imitation satin trim, an empress of straitened means.

G rowing up, I assumed illness was normal. Only when I began to hear about friends' families did I realize that they took health for granted.

My childhood trained me to see the wince hidden under the public face. It made me aware of how much ordinary pain there is in the world, made me question why so universal an experience is so little acknowledged.

We need new words for illness, not to be drawn from the lexicon of complaint or from the book of invalidating phrases: Have I used up my 'sick days'? Am I sick enough?

Sorry, I'm a little 'off' today.

Get better.

We need subtle words that allow for degrees between healthy and sick, descriptive words for naming the in-between states where we spend much of our lives. We obscure these states with silence, or catchalls – 'I'm not feeling well' – but our lives are more complex. They ask not for confession, but for calibration, so that we may tell one another how we are.

We need a new language for pain so we don't experience it as simply a message delivered by an insulted nerve. Instead, the message is made up of a vocabulary of singular words that, when near one another, let us read pain as a story of all that has happened in our lives.

The phone rings. I jump up to answer it: a relative wanting to know where she should send flowers. I stand in my parents' kitchen chatting, not too happily but wanting to keep my end up. This one's a talker. 'I have to get off now, but thanks so much, I know my mother will be pleased.' Ha! She'll say, 'That one only calls when there's trouble.'

My father is sitting opposite me at breakfast, his hairy shoulders sticking out from his undershirt like fenders on an old car. Out of nowhere he begins to yell at me in a tone that a hack driver might use toward a recalcitrant horse. 'There is one thing I'm going to get you to do, no matter what!'

I say nothing. Inside I feel like a rebellious adolescent.

'Your mother's the same way! When you talk on the phone, you sit. Not stand. You hear me? You and your mother are the same. Chairs are for sitting. I'm training her . . . and you're going to do the same thing.'

I'm open-mouthed. Then: 'No I am not. I stand when I speak on the phone. You are not training me. Okay? Understood?'

I phone my Aunt Minna, who says, 'He's never been able to handle frustration. And it's worse now that he's had the strokes. Please, don't take it personally.'

My father has fallen asleep in the big electrically powered chair that tilts downward so that he can ease himself out of it. It is dark in the room, save for the lights of Boston spread over the hills. In the morning, he likes to stand at this window, watching the sun come up.

Out of the blue, my father says, 'I was just watching that stupid film, The Battle of Waterloo . . . war, it's so stupid . . . why do people want to kill each other?'

Another night, I come in and he's sitting in the dark.

'I don't know about getting old. Is it worth it?'

Another night: 'What's it all about? Who knows?'

Me: 'I do.'

Just to give him some kind of answer.

He'd wake me early in the morning, before school, to go with him to buy meat for his grocery store. In the old market at Faneuil Hall, we'd walk down aisles, between haunches hanging from hooks. My father would greet the butchers, stopping to exchange a few friendly words.

'This is my daughter.'

'Spitting image, huh Lou?'

They all wore thick gloves and knitted mufflers except for my father. He was the Good Guy; he also tried to be the Strong Guy.

'Gloves? What do I need them for? I can't feel a damn thing; I've got my own lard.'

They'd chuckle; one of the men would give him a fake rabbit punch to his belly. Then he'd change his voice to the serious, mellifluous tone he thought appropriate for men doing business and inquire about the union boss or the price of lamb.

At the end of an aisle, we'd come to a large wooden door with a steel spring latch. When the door swung open, the inside sent out steam, like breath makes on a cold day. My father took me around to the shelves lining the walls, pointing out sections where cuts were kept, different grades of ribs, legs, shoulders. We'd stay in the freezer for as long as we could, until my father would say, 'Okay, babe, we've had enough.'

B ack in California, I put off phoning my parents for a few days. I don't want to lessen my joy at being home. Cool air comes through the bedroom window, washing over Steve's and my happy bodies. Eucalyptus seed capsules have lodged in the screen, sending out a pungent fragrance. I enjoy the heft of my own coffee mug. Our dog runs to retrieve his orange plush carrot.

I got lucky fifteen years ago. After some bad years – divorce, cancer, a dead-end job – I met my husband, a brilliant and kind man. Right from the start, we've been crazy about each other, happy talking about ideas, enjoying each other's minds, happy also going to a delicatessen, sitting in a booth and watching a Lakers game.

Until I met him, I hadn't understood the concept of a good match. I thought a romantic relationship was based on one person filling what the other lacks, a notion that should carry a warning against change. Steve and I fit. I felt tenderness early in our courtship, when he stood in the shower soaping his hair, all the while earnestly explaining to me how a weather system works.

Twelve years ago Steve was offered the presidency of California Institute of the Arts. Since then I've been part of a community of artists committed to experimental work and uncompromising questioning. When we arrived, the college was in bad shape; six years later, we clinked our glasses on New Year's Eve, toasting the fact that the school was now creatively and financially safe. Two weeks later, an earthquake decimated the campus, leaving us forty million dollars in debt.

I'm not sure we would have stayed at CalArts all these years had we not been engaged in a life-and-death effort to rebuild. Disaster bonded us, or, more accurately, getting through it and prevailing. We were tested, and it has kept us linked.

The CalArts residence, a spacious house surrounded by grounds used for college events, is now filled with our books and art, exotic objects from our travels, postcards from friends on the refrigerator door. In the garage, an enormous puppet stands almost as high as the roof; mounted on a steel frame, it had been carried aloft by students to celebrate a new theater we're building.

It's the variety, and most of all, the spirit of our lives, that gives me joy. At first, I was afraid to drive the freeways. Now I'm a cowgirl, riding my car through canyons and mountain passes, taking the curves with ease.

When I do call, my mother seems to be doing a little better, but my father has lost ground, erupting at the slightest disturbance.

'Your father's been terrible, he blames me for the least little thing, he yells at me all the time . . .'

It's not something she mentions often, but when she does I feel awful for her.

'Would it be any use if I talked to him?'

'No.'

What do I imagine? I'll say 'Do it for me,' and he will? He may not be able to stop himself.

On the way home from the hospital, he had wanted me to let him out at a red light, on the passenger side where he'd step into a line of cars about to move. 'It's not a good idea, Dad, with the cane and all . . .' He started to open the door, but I was too fast for him; from my side, I switched on the lock on his door. 'Let me out of here,' he said through his teeth. 'I am not letting you out into traffic.' 'Get me out,' he yelled, rattling the door handle.

My mother has seen far worse. A few years ago after a hip operation, anesthesia made him crazy. He went raging through the hospital floor threatening to hurt other patients. It was so bad we thought he'd have to go to a psychiatric ward.

During a quiet moment, I stood beside him in his room.

'I don't have my glasses; what's that number on the wall?'

'Dad, there aren't any numbers on the wall.'

Seeing him become increasingly frustrated by my failure to see the obvious, I changed tactics.

'The one in the middle is an eight.'

My mother, visiting him every day, brought offerings for the nurses – boxes of donuts, jars of jelly beans. She listened to their problems, offered advice, sent me index cards with their favorite recipes. She told them stories from years of married life, so they'd see him not as a madman but as a beloved husband.

Her efforts paid off. Little by little he regained his sanity until one day a nurse, recognizing his return to himself, caroled, 'Lou is back!'

In a neurologist's terms, what's the big deal about a few ordinary delusions, a few common losses? But the changes in my father felt unbearable to me. Worst was when he had a fixed idea – not exactly an obsession but an intransigent belief in what he thought was right, what should happen in the face of all evidence to the contrary.

He wanted to solve a problem for me: where to park my rental car in a neighborhood whose spaces were zoned for residents. In his mind, a rental car should be exempt from such stipulations. A fine idea, but not the case. I questioned both the rental agency and the building manager so I could give him a definitive answer, which he refused to accept. He'd shake his head in exasperation and say, 'I don't understand,' or, 'Are you sure?'

He could do this twenty times in as many minutes. Either he forgot each time or had once learned a different answer that kept asserting itself so that my information seemed counterintuitive. Or the strokes had impaired his ability to learn, not so much to comprehend as to be satisfied with comprehension. Or perhaps it's not about learning. Maybe we're engaged in a battle between competing ideas of what life, if it were fair, would offer.

We were pleased, the three of us, to be invited to the opening of a new meat processing plant. I invited a friend from the fourth grade to come with us.

My parents didn't know the other guests. Most of them were from the wholesale side of the business. We were retail. At one end of the reception hall was a buffet table loaded with platters of meat laid out in pinwheels. In the center, people milled around, a little lost in the big space.

My father's repeated trips to the buffet for stacks of pink bologna gave him a destination. My mother stood by herself waiting for him to come back; with her nervous stomach she couldn't eat the food, but she was gratified at being the recipient of largesse.

My friend and I sped off to explore the building, the size of an entire block, filled with gleaming new machinery that had been shown to us earlier on a tour of the plant. We climbed stairs to an unused top floor, lit only by a few windows and the outline of light at the edges of a closed door. A few steps led up to the door; it wasn't locked.

Blinding in the sunlight, the roof emitted an odor so fierce we took a step back and ran, holding our noses, which had already taken in a bitter brown smell. We'd seen something dark and disgusting spread over the entire surface of the roof.

We caught up with my father on a return trip from the buffet, his plate stacked, a large dollop of Gulden's mustard and a Parker House roll on the side. We told him what we'd seen on the roof.

My father headed over to where several men were talking together. Standing behind, my dad tapped one on the shoulder.

'Joe,' he said.

The man turned around. In the white shirt and tie of a boss, this was the man who'd been our guide for the tour. His eyes registered uncertainty: who was this man, laden with food and two little girls? He was courteous, though, as he informed us the factory also brewed beer. It had been the hops we'd smelled, drying on the roof. He turned back to his conversation.

'Joe's a good man,' my dad said. 'I told you he'd know.'

We started back to my mother. I walked with care; my father had given me the job of bringing her a cup of tea. For himself, he took a glass filled with Moxie, the soft drink so strong that swallowing it down was a badge of bravado.

She's home now, convalescent. 'All I want is to be left alone. I've gone through a lot, and if you want to know the truth, I don't care about anything.'

I picture her standing at the phone. For a second, I see not my own mother but my grandmother, her upper lip lined like piecrust dough pressed by the tines of a fork.

'No one calls; no one comes over.'

'But how can you complain when you won't let anyone do anything for you?'

She's quiet for a moment.

'People are selfish. I know you think it's different. And it is different for you. In California you have friends, people whose parents live far away, people who are all alone, and you help each other. But not here. This is a cold, cold city. Here you're alone.'

Now she seems so young to me. I've traveled where she has not been; she has stayed in Boston with the order she has managed to amass – the apartment where every year she has climbed on a stool, opening each ring on the curtain rod, gathering the heavy drapes in her arms, soaking them a pair at a time in the tub, days of ironing . . . and rehanging them, turned and pinned and smoothed to hide the faded parts. She hears of California as a queen might have listened to an explorer, wanting not foreign gifts but another's eyes to see the gleaming room that surrounds her, the clean, green drapes – praise for the effort and cost and will to maintain.

'I have to be realistic. In the end you're alone.'

Is this her idea of wisdom?

'But you're not alone – '

She remembers we're talking long distance. 'We have to hang up,' she says. 'Do you have any idea of what this call is going to cost you?'

Tests have made it official. After several episodes of small transient strokes, my father has suffered brain damage.

I don't know what to do with myself. It's as though grief were spilling like water over a dam, generating energy.

We keep a ping-pong table on a patio out in back. I'd like to slam some balls back and forth, but there's no one around. Then I spot Ruth, mowing the lawn over on the other side of the house. She's a gardener sent by the college to take care of the grounds.

I'm hesitant to talk with her; she keeps her distance. To her, I'm a boss who could cause her to lose her job. Better to stay away, which is what I think too. What if I said something she'd tell everyone about back at the college?

I make my way across a swath of lawn big enough to hold parties for the entire college. I shout over the noise of the mower.

'Ruth.'

She's a hefty, taciturn woman, the kind that used to be called a 'bottle blonde.' She can't hear me.

'Ruth!'

She switches off the mower.

'I just heard some bad news about my father. Would you be able to stop work for a few minutes and maybe play Ping-Pong with me?'

She says, no, she has to get all the pyracanthas cleared out today.

Okay. Right. I must have been crazy.

I go into the house. The books, the maps, the postcards from friends . . . everywhere there are visible signs of solace. The rooms we inhabit, the objects we surround ourselves with, the words we write – what are these if not a highly articulated set of consolations? Then something happens, and I'm inconsolable.

'He's my husband. It happened to him . . . it could have happened to any of us.'

My mother goes on. 'It's not his fault. Underneath he's a sweet, loving man, and the man I married . . .'

To overlook faults and failings, to offer love when it's not being given: this I believe is goodness.

But my father wasn't a sweet man when he raged at us to get out of the car, not once but many times. He wasn't the pussycat she liked to call him when he screamed at her for no reason. Once he broke my favorite record album over his knee, tearing Nat King Cole's smile in two. Is it better to forget such things?

My mother overlooks other sides of my father's nature, and it lets her cope. But isn't the price too high? It means losing more complex truths.

23

'You analyze too much,' she has always said to me. 'You can't take everything apart.'

But it has always been my way to understand. I think we're given little windows of time between difficulties, openings that hold out a promise of clarity. We need to acknowledge such grace periods and use them for deeper scrutiny.

But why, deep down under the surface where I imagine it can't be detected, am I dismissive of people who won't risk scrutiny? What is clarity, anyway? Perhaps it's the mercy of deeper love?

Oh there's brain damage in the east, and brain damage in the west, and upstairs there's brain damage and downstairs there's brain damage, and in my lady's parlor – brain damage.

I read these words years ago, in Donald Barthelme's then just-published book *City Life*. Why do I remember them? Is it the rhythm, the little foxtrot? Or was memory acting as precursor – not exactly a forecast, more of an inchoate knowledge based on hint and fear of my father's future condition?

I begin to read about the brain. My husband says I undertake research as a way to cope. He's right. But I maintain that my interest is more than a coping mechanism. Knowledge is also the lure, the pursuit of it as on a trail, ears perking, nose twitching, sniffing closer to the earth until I pick up a first strong scent and then the slow aromatic release of meaning.

There's so much that's new since the days when I was a philosophy major. The neurological entwining of emotion and reason! Biology, mind, and culture all interacting! Body and mind inseparable! I feel as if I'm stuffed to bursting with new ideas.

Note to myself on the computer: 'Calm, calm, you are not a sausage . . .'

My mind is becoming populated: first by a famous figure of neurology, Phineas Gage, a young man of 'temperate habits' and 'considerable energy of character.' In 1848, Gage was a construction foreman, working on laying down new tracks for a railroad across stony Vermont. He was preparing to blast some solid rock when, with the force of an explosive, a three-foot-long tamping iron, a tool made to his specifications, pierced his cheek, angled through his brain, and flew out of his skull.

To everyone's surprise, many of his faculties survived intact; it was his character that suffered. The damage to his frontal lobes had changed him. As his physician wrote, 'the balance . . . between his intellectual faculty and animal propensities' had been destroyed. His friends said sadly, 'Gage isn't Gage anymore.'

Next, a woman stepped forward from the neurological literature: Madame I, identified by her initial in a case history. Madame I was twenty-eight years old in 1905, when researchers began to study her. She had come to Salpêtrière Hospital after wandering Paris in a confused state, weeping and trying to undress herself. She attributed her problems to the violent character of her husband.

When Madame I's confusion abated, she fell into a state she described as 'general insensibility.' She couldn't feel her body; it didn't exist for her. 'I'm no longer aware of myself as I used to be. I can no longer feel my arms, my legs, my head and my hair . . . when I speak, I no longer hear the sound of my own voice . . . It is as if I were dead.'

The news is bad. The bypass didn't work; there's almost no cir-culation in her leg.

'Why am I being punished? All my life, I've tried so hard to be good.'

'You should be proud; you did the right thing, the brave thing.'

'For what?'

What can I say?

In all honesty?

I tell her she has been good all her life, that she is good and should be proud of it.

I can't tell her that her goodness will hold her in good stead.

I wish I could tell her my own belief, that there's a force in the universe, chaotic and impersonal, that doesn't add, nor check, nor reward. She has built her life on trying. But for whom? The approval of the father who abandoned his family, of the mother who stinted with her love? Is this what spurs us on, to be good in God's eyes or in the eyes of those other gods, our fellow humans, and so become beloved?

Before I go to Boston, I read a book a friend has given me, a Buddhist text on compassion that describes a breathing practice of focusing on someone else's suffering, taking it inside oneself in order to breathe out relief. I'm afraid to take my mother's suffering inside me; I'm afraid that once inside, it will stay there.

I count on my accomplishments, my helpfulness, to make me feel that I'm a good person. But all of that has come easily compared to now, when what I need is largeness of heart. I don't know how to expand my heart.

On the plane, I jot down something from the book, a phrase made new by being given a Buddhist twist: DON'T JUST DO SOMETHING – SIT THERE. I stick the note inside my eyeglass case so I can't help seeing it when I'm in Boston.

A row of pay phones lines the hospital lobby wall. People lean into the cubicles, separated from one another by partitions so thin they can't help overhearing each other's troubles. I'm bonded to them by a fellow feeling that springs up in places where people wait, as now, while operations are in progress.

At last. The surgeon comes up from the operating room, smiling, congenial, spiffy in a navy blazer and khaki pants. This is the man who a few minutes ago cut off my mother's leg. He says the operation went well. He was able to remove her right leg below the knee, one of the two sites where amputation is done. It is the preferred place; she could have lost the leg mid-thigh. He says there could eventually be a problem with her good leg, but we just have to hope nothing bad will happen.

Now that the waiting is over, I don't know what to do with myself. Over a cup of coffee from the lobby dispenser, I start wondering where the leg went. I try to censor this thought, labeling it a leftover from a pretentious novel. I do not want to be thinking about this, but I can't seem to shut it out. Do they just throw the leg away? Do they incinerate it?

I know my mother's foot very well. It is a foot quite unlike my own, which is more like my father's. Narrow mother toes, nailbeds narrow too. More elegant than mine. Good bones in her foot. Good legs, for that matter, which she didn't show off but could have.

Could have. Didn't.

Didn't have the confidence for the last ten years or so to go out without that wig. While she's still in the recovery room, I follow her instructions to go to her room and put the wig back on the head. I dutifully deliver it to the apartment, replacing it on a tray table in her closet.

Without the wig, my mother is beautiful. Thin gray hairs, my hand smoothing them away from her brow. Soft skin, still. Her finely articulated bones under my fingers. Her silver hair streams back from a high hairline. Her thin nose arches like a ballerina's foot on point. My mother resembles a Russian dancer, one of the old ones who become teachers and stand in class beside a piano, beating time.

With your toe, go tap tap tap, With your hand go clap clap clap, Round about and hm hm hm? Turn around and once again.

Each little girl took a few steps right and stopped, put her foot in the center and tapped three times, then made a quarter turn and clapped the upraised hands of the girl next to her. My mother in her Brownie leader uniform led us through the song.

Later, I will fly up and be a Girl Scout myself: at my installation ceremony, I will recite Emma Lazarus's poem by heart; I will go on to get my writer's badge. Later too, I will come to see my mother as pinched, a killjoy, her abilities nipped. For a while, I will put aside my memories of her great day.

In Boston Garden, where the Celtics used to play, my mother led the Girl Scout leaders of America, two by two, marching into the center of the basketball court, where she mounted a podium and gave the speech she'd written about the ideals of Scouting. I'd seen her covering pages of stationery, fountain pen in hand. She'd been picked by organizers of the annual conference to represent troop leaders from around the nation. Before her speech, we all rose and recited the Juliette Lowe Pledge. I know this because I've kept the program.

She'd been so nervous beforehand, sick with it. But that day no one knew; she spoke confidently, in a firm sweet voice. I sat proudly in the bleachers wearing my Scout uniform, following her words as the lights of the Garden shone on her.

I'm afraid to look. As the visiting nurse starts to unwrap my mother's bandage, I avert my eyes, look for somewhere else to focus.

A few days before the operation, her leg had become a thick tube, hot and pink, the skin pulled taut, and waxy as though covered with a caul. The first time I saw her lying in bed with one leg ending in a stump, I couldn't believe it. A few minutes later I looked again, and I believed it.

But when she began to move her leg under a sheet and it looked as though a creature from a science fiction movie was making its way across the bed, this I do not get used to, not a few days after the operation, not now.

'Rub it, not too nicely,' the nurse says. 'Slap it until it becomes callused, like an elbow.'

She must sense that I, the visiting daughter, disapprove because she tells me this is regular practice: amputees are routinely instructed to slap their stumps in order to stimulate a phantom limb.

Why would anyone in her right mind want a phantom limb? She doesn't answer; that's not her job. But from my reading, I know the answer. A phantom limb turns out to be essential for walking. When a prosthesis is strapped on, the phantom shoots out and 'fills' it. The brain then begins to accept the artificial leg as though it were part of the body, able to be used for walking.

There's also a bad phantom that mysteriously appears to some amputees but not to others, the one that causes my mother to say, 'Right now as we're talking, a corn I had on my little toe is killing me.' Sometimes she feels as though a red-hot poker were scalding the leg that's not there.

Her first prosthesis was a heavy contraption of metal and straps given to her after surgery. Its advantage, besides providing extra support, was that it allowed for a gap so the stump didn't have to rest directly against a surface. I tried picking it up and couldn't believe how heavy it was. I don't know how she even managed to lift her leg with that thing strapped on.

The hospital has now given her a much lighter one, covered with a thin layer of spongy stuff and ending in one of her own shoes. Sometimes, though, she needs the original one because her stump isn't healing as fast as the doctor would like. I wonder about these legs; the toes and nails look so much like her own. I ask my mother if they'd made a cast of her foot.

'How could they?' she replies, 'The foot was gone.'

Most of the time my mother doesn't wear either artificial leg, but she keeps both close by just in case. The apartment seems filled with them. They move around a lot: a leg against the sink, a leg propped against the kitchen counter, a leg leaning against the aluminum railing that helps her get up from the toilet.

My mother asks if I could please bring her the light leg. The heavy leg is now in the back of a closet, serving as a receptacle in which to store rolls of gift-wrapping paper. The light leg I can't seem to locate; it's not in the den, nor do I see it in the living room on the machine-woven oriental rug, which is the only place it could be. My mother would never tolerate it on the velvet sofa or the wing chair.

I take a quick look at myself in a mirror. Behind me is a wall of Impressionist paintings, reproductions my mother hung in the style of a European art gallery. How she came by her taste is a mystery. She never traveled or studied, but somehow she learned the language of rose medallion, sarouk, and majolica. She must have seen period rooms at the Boston Museum of Fine Arts, where she describes herself as crouching behind an Egyptian sarcophagus so the guards wouldn't spot her, a little girl eating a sandwich from home. I've heard this story a number of times, including the detail that the sandwich was chicken salad. It's one of those mysteries that in a family remain legend, unavailable for inquiry. Why didn't she walk outside with her sandwich? Why did she go to the museum in the first place? What need for beauty brought her there? And why a sarcophagus? Why chicken salad?

The leg's not in the bedroom either, although there's that huge portrait of me above my parents' bed, placed so they can see its reflection in the mirror on the opposite wall. Originally it had been a black-and-white studio photograph, but in the style of the time it had been painted over to resemble an oil painting. I hated that image of a chubby little girl in a blue puff-sleeved dress, hands neatly folded in her lap, serene smile belying intense feelings. I told visitors she was my twin sister who had died.

To my parents the portrait was a marvel; they'd proudly point out how the eyes would follow someone walking across the room. When I was in high school, the portrait's fate was placed in my hands. A cleaning woman, thinking the picture had become dirty, washed it with a solvent that removed the color. My parents gave me a choice: leave it the way it was, or have it restored? I knew their need was stronger than mine. I chose for them.

I find the leg in the bathroom and carry it to her in what I find is the easiest position, shoe sole resting on my interlaced fingers, leg upright against my chest. In Holy Week processions in Spain, the faithful carry their crosses in a similar way. Steve and I once saw a father and son in Seville, the two of them waiting together for a bus on a sunny afternoon. The father was already dressed for that night's procession, wearing a long robe with a pointed hood and rope belt. Below the robe his high-top sneakers were visible. In one arm, the father shouldered the Cross; with the other arm, he held his son by the elbow, keeping him safely away from the path of an oncoming bus. Tonight I'm a solo procession, a daughter who protects her parents, walking not to a cathedral but to the dining room.

In a Back Bay mansion converted to doctors' offices, my mother and I ascended in an ornate cage big enough only for two. The elevator rose alongside a sweeping marble staircase. My mother remarked on the beauty of its curve, the fine oriental rug that ran down its center.

The eminent pediatrician examined me and said that the pains in my ankles were nothing more than an excuse to stay home from the first grade. I was making it up.

A thorough doctor, he ordered a blood test just in case. I remember something that can't be true and yet . . . a vial in the shape of an hourglass standing on a mantlepiece in the doctor's waiting room. My mother and I sat there while my blood dripped all the way down.

Was I really sick? Or was I just looking for attention?

My mother and aunts competed for the attention illness brings; their crazy brother, Herbie, had taken it all away from them. We children were enlisted. Did a cousin have whooping cough? I had to have a worse case.

A little bell rang, calling us back into the doctor's office. He said I had rheumatic fever. For a year or so, I had to be carried from room to room. I had a home tutor. I read *Tales from Shakespeare, The Door in the Wall, Little Women*. I imagined Hermione on her pedestal, Robin on his horse, Beth on her deathbed. In the middle of the twentieth century, I was having a nineteenth-century childhood.

Sol Snyder bent over me with his dyed black hair, natty checked sports jacket, and breath that smelled as though he'd sprayed it with medicine, the way a doctor should smell.

He straightened up and pronounced, 'Rheumatic fever.'

The problem was that Sol wasn't a real doctor.

'It wasn't his fault he went to Suffolk,' my mother used to say. 'It was cheap, and his family didn't have a cent. But it never got accredited, so some people look down their noses at Sol. But he's our friend; I know he'll come to the house when we need him.'

Did I have rheumatic fever again, nine years after the first time? Or did I need Sol to give me license to stay home from high school and read *Crime and Punishment* under the covers?

One thing about my aunts, they always knew how to behave in an illness. When I was little, my mother's sister Pauline came bringing magical presents. An iced cake with satin ribbons attached to tiny gifts baked inside. A wicker basket with strawberries nestling in a pretty floral cloth. With the berries would come the story of when she was sick as a little girl.

'My mother knew I adored strawberries. Even if she didn't have a penny to her name, she'd find a way to get me some.'

My mother stood in the doorway, thumbs tucked in, lips clamped. After Pauline left, I was given to understand that her stories were fabrications, embroideries on the truth or worse.

'She just wants to prove that my mother loved her best.'

From what I can gather, my mother's judgment was correct. Pauline's memories were fictions, a means for drawing attention to her superior claims. But I thought there was something to be said for a happy story, especially if it had been made up.

Years later, in the hospital recovering from a mastectomy, I phoned my parents and pretended I was calling from a hotel room in Puerto Rico.

Eventually I had to tell them the truth. I braced myself to hear a cry; I'd met the family's fate.

Instead, my mother replied, 'I am a lionness, and you are my cub.'

Two years later, though, when I had a recurrence, I didn't mention it to my parents. Why worry them when it hadn't metastasized? When it was only the original pathology briefly reasserting itself?

'Max got all the good genes,' laughs my mother's sister Minna, speaking of her own great-uncle, who at ninety became the oldest person ever to receive a graduate degree from Harvard. 'Now there was an intact brain,' Minna says, comparing, or so I think, Max with the lobotomized end of the family spectrum.

'I have weak brains,' Minna laughs. 'That's what the boarder used to say, the crazy one who sat in my mother's kitchen all day long arguing with the Jewish newspaper. When he'd catch sight of me, that's what he'd say, "Minna, the trouble with you is you have weak brains."'

No, the comparison was with herself. When Minna left school to go to work after the eighth grade, she confided to Max that she wanted to be a writer.

Max, always practical, said 'Minna, why don't you wait?' She did, for the rest of her life.

I inherited what Minna calls the family's writing gene. Legend has it the gene was passed on by the revered Max, who was still able at ninety to recall the taste of a berry he'd plucked while riding in the cart that was taking him away from Russia. On the strength of that recollected berry, I thought of him as the writer in the family. Eventually I came to see that it was Minna who was a storyteller, and I a child poet, seeing in my mind's eye an orange berry dangling from a black branch.

In the seventh and eighth grades, I learned about poetry at Girls' Latin School, a Boston public school that required a stiff qualifying test. In its corridors and classrooms, I was with girls whose only common feature was love of learning. I took pleasure in scanning poetry, at ease with my love of trochees and my lesser love of iambs, and my fondness for their relatives, the dactyl, which made me think of vast wings attached to a lizard body, and anapest, which I imagined as a city in eastern Europe.

Girls' Latin taught me to diagram complex sentences and translate Cicero. In a yearlong science course whose semesters neatly paired geology and astronomy, I committed to memory the diameter and circumference of all the islands in Boston Harbor. I also had to memorize comparable figures for all the then-known planets in the solar system. Of course I haven't remembered a single measurement; what I do recall is that islands in my hometown waters were hinged to outer space.

In Minna's back room, I discovered Auden's elegy to a fellow poet.

Earth, receive an honored quest
William Yeats is laid to rest.

It was the beat that got me, that trochaic tread, stately, processional, that ushered in history itself. To this day when I hear those lines in my head, I feel something in me stirring.

Until then, the past was too close, taking shape in refugees brought here by Jewish relief organizations. Mrs. Landsman had lost her children in Auschwitz; once a week she would come to our house to clean, although we weren't in a position to afford a cleaning woman and my mother always worked alongside her. They'd wash floors on their hands and knees, sharing a soapy bucket. My mother was pretty and stylish. Mrs. Landsman wore a housedress that smelled of steam and sweat; over her hair she tied a scarf as red as her face. Her Yiddish was guttural, her voice shrill. Later that evening, my mother would say, 'We washed the floor with our tears.'

I knew I should pity Mrs. Landsman for what had happened to her. Instead, I felt that if this is the past, get me away from it, its smell, its suds, its mournfulness.

But when I read Auden's elegy, I pictured cold bridges over curved rivers, people huddled in dark coats as they waited for streetcars that would take them out beyond the city limits where they lived in 'ranches of isolation.' This Europe was overrun by murderous hordes that only a bardic voice could keep at bay.

> Follow, poet, follow right
> to the bottom of the night.

I heard the imperative in the trochee. Do it. Make it.

> With your unconstraining voice
> Still persuade us to rejoice.

At those moments, I sprang free of my own history. No longer a solitary little girl, I was part of a great line in which I myself might become an honored poet.

But what, I wondered, did Auden mean when he wrote, 'Mad Ireland hurt you into poetry?' I knew that Auden was speaking of a madness very different from what I saw when my mother took me to visit my uncle. Yeats's Ireland was a place where passions ruled, whose sovereign was a poet whose words could survive it all. In my own house, I stood on a chair waving my arms, conducting an invisible orchestra of poetry.

M y cousin makes it clear; she'd rather I not ask her mother any questions.

'She's an old woman,' Ellie says. 'Hasn't she earned the right to be left alone?'

But Minna is wiser than her daughter; she knows I'm not inquiring for any hurtful use. Besides, Ellie's the one who has said, 'I've tried to shield my children from knowledge of the past,' by which she means the family's history of mental illness.

I don't agree with her. Her children have become adults; I hope they know more than she thinks. That's a belief that belongs to my generation. Writers hunt for old diaries left in attics, filmmakers for footage stored and forgotten in basements. We pry open lids, convinced that secrets must be brought to light. We go on questioning until we elicit that one response that inspires us: 'Why do you want to know?'

Because Herbie would open the door of the apartment where he lived with my grandmother, his eyes dull, unchanging when he saw my mother and Minna. With exaggerated cadences, as though courting a shy child, they'd greet their middle-aged brother. 'How nice you look, Herbie,' one of them would say, exclaiming at a recent haircut or a new sweater vest. Sometimes he'd greet me with a tiny upturning of lips that signified a smile under duress. He'd cup a hand around my ear, his fingers reaching to the back, behind the rim. It was an attempt at a friendly gesture; I knew that. But the touch of his limp fingers felt awful. His shirt was always buttoned to the neck. When he put his glasses on, it was with both hands, positioning the wire rims over both ears. To this day, I can't stand seeing a man wear a shirt buttoned all the way up. I can't bear to have anyone fondle my ear. When I put on my own eyeglasses with both hands I am, for the flash of a second, Herbie.

Meanwhile, Minna's game. As she points out, she's in her nineties, so what more is there not to talk about?

'It's a good time; the news is over. Hold on, we'll go into the kitchen.' Eyeglasses, apron, pearls – I picture her walking into the kitchen and seating herself at the table, where there are always cups and saucers at the ready.

'At the beginning, what made you know Herbie was sick?'

'There were signs. He seemed bright. Then he started to do things that were "off." He threw a cat over a third floor railing. But no one understood. Not like now. Then he became violent. The doctors said he had dementia praecox, which was what they used to call schizophrenia. In those days they didn't know how to treat people like Herbie, so he went into the State Hospital, which was a terrible place. The conditions were beyond belief. We knew that. Everyone knew.

'Herbie never stayed long. Each time he was committed, my mother would get him out. She'd throw a fit in front of the attendants. "Help me," she'd cry, and then she'd faint. I saw it all because I was the oldest and she needed me to sign his release papers.'

'How could Grandma keep him at home?'

'Nobody else mattered; she was obsessed. Herbie was always first.'

'But he was violent, wasn't he?'

'He terrified all of us, especially Francie. She was the youngest, so she was in the house with him. Your mother was in high school, and I was already working. We were scared too, but we made excuses for my mother.'

'What did you think when a lobotomy was suggested?'

'We didn't think. You can't imagine how ignorant we were. A doctor told us we wouldn't have to be so scared, that it would pacify Herbie. After the operation, he didn't talk for ten years. He just sat in a chair with the television on, maybe with a magazine on his lap, but we didn't know whether he could read.'

As Minna talks, I feel the scratchy fabric of that armchair, the crocheted doilies on the armrests, damp after he got up.

'One day I was standing on the back porch with him. He said something about a little girl playing in the yard; she was wearing the same hair ribbon as the day before.'

'I couldn't believe my ears. I think I said something like, "Yes, that's right, Herbie." I was afraid to say the wrong thing.'

'When I was a kid, he'd never shut up.'

'That was later. It turned out all that time he'd been taking things in, what he'd seen in television and magazines. It got all mixed up in that poor brain of his. He thought Harry Truman was pestering him; that was one of the ideas he couldn't get out of his mind. On the way to the barbershop, he'd turn around in the middle of the sidewalk and shake his finger at someone. People would take offense. They didn't know he was scolding Truman.'

2   A disease is never a mere loss or excess – there is always a reaction, on the part of the affected organism or individual, to restore, to replace, to compensate for and to preserve its identity, however strange the means may be.

Oliver Sacks

M adame I had been at Salpêtrière Hospital for two years, re-
maining in the same state. In bed, she could not tell where her
legs were. When her mouth was shut, she could not find her tongue.

During that time, neurologists G. Denys and P. Camus studied her
case. In their published report, they quoted Madame I: 'People and
things appear like phantoms . . . I can imagine neither my parents,
nor the interior of the house . . . I have forgotten the tastes of food,
the scent of flowers, and the voices of my children.'

The neurologists wrote that her physical difficulties, while considerable, seemed to cause her less suffering than her emotional state.
She was profoundly troubled by the loss of her own existence.
'Madame I is perfectly clearheaded,' they concluded. 'At moments
when she is not dominated by her anxiety, she helps other patients,
reads, and sews. But most of the time she tries to recover her lost
sensibility.'

'Where's your other half?' a friend asked Steve when he saw him alone at a concert.

'She's back in Boston again; her mother's been ill.'

'What's wrong?'

When Steve explained, his friend introduced one of the guests in his box, a professor of neurology and an authority on phantom limb.

Dr. Fisher gave Steve his card and told him I would be welcome to call when I get back.

I set off for Dr. Fisher's office at UCLA, my head crammed, yellow pad full of questions.

Dr. Fisher is affable. On his desk are family photographs, on the wall a poster autographed by a cellist I also admire – good signs that we'll like each other. He gives me an overview of why someone can feel pain in a part of the body that's not there.

'We know that the experience of a phantom limb has the quality of reality because it's produced by the same brain processes that underlie the experience of the body when it's intact.

'But we don't know why some people feel only the presence of a phantom limb, while for others, like your mother, it's excruciatingly painful. I don't want to dash any hopes you might have about her condition,' Dr. Fisher goes on, 'but there are so many areas where we just don't know answers.'

'Will it go away?'

'Sometimes yes, sometimes no. It can go away for years and then come back. How long did your mother have severe pain, when she still had her leg?'

'Three years.'

'That's bad. There's a theory that pain felt after an amputation is more or less the same pain that the patient felt before losing the limb. It makes sense; the neurological pathways in and out of the brain were laid down in the past, so they may well go right on carrying old impulses. Because your mother has had a history of pain, her condition is likely to last a long while.'

'Can it disappear, once and for all?'

'No one knows . . . the phantom itself tends to fade or telescope and disappear as a function of time. But a phantom may return decades after it seems to be gone.'

'Is it a memory?'

'Physically, no – it's normal experience continuing as it must. It's the real thing, not a pathological entity. But, in a purely psychological sense, one could say it's the body's unwillingness to relinquish its past.'

The Sherman sisters – Minna, my mother, Jen, Pauline, and Francie – were sitting around Minna's living room, one or the other disappearing to make sure every last thing had been cleared up, the kitchen floor swept, husbands contentedly ensconced in the den. I stayed in the living room with its familar wallpaper of red cabbage roses. My mother and I were tanned; we'd just come back from summer at the beach.

'We'd go into a store,' Minna said with mild amusement, 'and my father would point to the first coat he saw. Whatever it looked like on me, he'd say, "We'll take it."'

My mother would break in. 'It didn't matter that it looked horrible. Or that I felt like a little ragamuffin, with sleeves coming down to my knees.'

Pauline, always her father's favorite, countered, 'Helen, you have to admit, Papa would fix the coat. He was a good tailor.'

'What did it matter? By then the damage was done,' my mother said bitterly. 'I was humiliated. The saleswomen were sorry for me; I could see it on their faces.'

Jen, the daring one, the one who as a teenager had climbed out a window to go dancing, asked, 'What would have happened if one of us had opened her mouth and said, "Pa, I don't like this coat?"'

'Are you out of your mind?' my mother snapped. 'You're living in a fantasy. If any of us dared to say one word to him, he'd rant and rave right there in the store.'

'You were so pretty, Helen,' said Minna, soothing the waters. 'You looked good no matter what you wore.'

My mother replied, 'Pauline was the pretty one. I was a little nothing.'

Driving he could do; in the cab he could be his own man. He loved taking people around Boston, showing them the sights off the meter.

'Go on,' my father said, enjoying his secret joke. We were facing a dead end street on Beacon Hill.

I walked up the steps of a wooden porch.

'Go on; don't be afraid.'

Beside the front door a light had been turned on. Lamplight shone through lace curtains.

I looked back at him.

'Is this okay?'

'Go on,' he insisted, 'look in the window.'

On tiptoe, I peered in. There was nothing there, no room, no furniture. I was flabbergasted. My father got a kick out of my double take. The false front was protection, he explained, so that people walking late at night – drunks, mostly, he added – wouldn't fall down the steep hill on the other side.

Once, the opera singer Lily Pons was his fare; he took her there too. My mother was impressed; she loved our recording of Pons singing 'The Bell Song' from Lakme.

I loved it all – Rowes Wharf, the barely risen biscuits at the No-Name Restaurant on Fish Pier, the ship's chandlery where they sold nautical instruments and wool sweaters with sheep's lanolin to keep fishermen warm.

Standing on a dock, my father explained the mysterious white hills that rose from a ship's deck. It was salt, brought to Boston from Venezuela. We watched as a nearby crane swung over the water and scooped up the salt, swinging back again to deposit it on the wharf. We saw the hills grow smaller as salt was needed for Boston's icy streets.

He made friends with Mrs. Kimball, the librarian at the Maritime Museum; once he brought me over to meet her at her apartment at the tip of the North End where you could see the water on three sides. I exclaimed at an old framed poster from a Dutch shipping line, three men in overalls, painted from the back as they leaned against a railing watching a ship come in. It was beautiful, with its soft yellows and oranges and light blue, the figures drawn in Daumier-like black outlines. Mrs. Kimball gave it to me, as I'd hoped she would; she knew I'd been admiring an image that evoked my father's world.

My father, the driver, the man who ferries his passengers. Each evening, my mother laid out a shirt and pair of pants on the couch in the den, along with freshly ironed boxer shorts and a ribbed undershirt. On wintry Boston days, she'd put a sweater vest there too, and thick-fingered wool-lined gloves that he'd never admit needing and would always leave behind. In the summer, the shirt was a light and comely plaid, short sleeves revealing his left forearm, deeply tanned from driving with the window down.

I'm relieved. After several months, my father is better, able to pick up prescriptions, do the grocery shopping. He no longer carries the big bags; they'll be delivered later, but he's at the door as he used to be, greeting me with his Who Did You Think It Was? grin.

He's able to solve problems for me, like the one I encounter when I wake up wet and sticky between my legs. After chemotherapy, which played havoc with my hormones, after tamoxifen, which put me into early menopause, after menopause itself, which surely should be well under way by now, I get my period. Of course I'm not carrying a tampon with me, so I have to improvise.

My father comes up with an elegant solution: that I use one of his Depends.

I feel like a version of Oedipus' riddle: What walks on two legs, inserts a pad between them in youth, later walks free again, only to return in age to the pad? Answer: A woman. What leaks blood and urine onto the same absorbent surface? Answer: A father and daughter.

Softly, so as not to wake him, I turn the key in the lock and tiptoe into the apartment. The light is still on in the hall, for my return. I go into the den, and my father's asleep on the daybed in his cotton pajamas, his head resting on his folded arm, looking like a young boy.

He stirs in his sleep, his movement taking me back to a walk with him in the North End. He had stopped dead in his tracks, cupping one hand to the side of his mouth while the other rested on the crook of a metal cane. His body swelled below his belt from an inoperable hernia and above from a brace that held his permanently fractured back in place, but when he shouted at the top of his lungs, his voice was still strong.

'Angela, Angela!'

I was worried as always that he'd erupt into a rage born of frustration, for he hadn't seen Angela since he retired, and she could well have moved away. For more than twenty years after the grocery store failed, he'd taken Angela in his yellow Checker cab to her job at the Registry of Motor Vehicles. She had been his regular fare, a single daughter who lived with her parents and was greeted every day by my father's interest in how her ailing mother was doing.

My father pointed across the street and sent me over to a building that might be hers. 'On the left, . . . read me the names.' At the top of the brick stoop, I called back to him, 'Giglio . . . McCann/Stewart . . .' not the one he was looking for.

'Angela,' he shouted again, and my worry was compounded. Would he be disappointed by this expedition to his old territory, where, as a child, I used to imagine him strolling the streets like the mayor of a small town in Sicily, greeting the barber, stopping to say hello to Mrs. Caggiano, the florist? I know now that mayor was wrong; I gave him a position and an authority he never had. He was an outsider, a friendly and obliging Jewish cab driver from another part of Boston who helped carry massive funeral wreaths out to the car and maneuvered a wheelchair down a steep stairway so that Angela's bedridden mother could get some air. On this night of return, would he be forced to see that his younger life is over?

He yelled up at another window in another building, his face getting more and more red. A little further up the street, my mother stood on the sidewalk, her shoulders rounding as though to protect herself from a blow. She would like nothing more than for him to cease, recognize that the past is gone, anything to stop that bellowing into vacancy.

'Sh-sh-sh . . .'

And I was in alliance with him once more, liking his capacity for action, his embrace of the past, and his ability to make noise, his appetites and desires, focused on that window. Up on the third floor, a curly gray head peered down, pure pleasure on her face, broad gums showing in a vast smile of welcome.

'Lou, Lou! I'll be right down.'

On the sidewalk they exchanged stories of Angela's new supervisor, her friend Marianne who had moved away to Charlestown, 'You remember her, Lou.'

Angela had lost a lot of weight. My mother complimented her, reminding her of when she couldn't fit into the black dress she kept for family funerals.

Angela beamed at the three of us who had shown up so unexpectedly at her door. Innocent of guile, she said to my mother, 'You had him, but I had him too.'

I shut off his bedside light and tiptoe into the kitchen to make a cup of decaf coffee, using the mug he was given when he worked at a shipping company after retiring from the cab company. He had a little business, Document and Shipping Service, using his own car to take messages, deliver bankrolls, ferry sick sailors to the hospital. The mug is oversized, with a drawing of a ship leading to a truck leading to a plane, a graphic tribute to a time earlier in the century when goods and services traveled through a Newtonian worldview: gears, levers, one thing lifted from one conveyance to another, one thing clearly resulting in another.

I sip my coffee in the darkened living room. I leave tomorrow. My mother's skin has become so thin that it tries to close but can't hold together. She needs frequent treatment from rotating nurses and physical therapists, who, I imagine, see her as a nice old woman. They'll never glimpse the little girl who used to be hoisted onto the kitchen table to sing for her family when the family was still intact, before her father left, before Herbie got sick. I picture her standing there, pleased and shy, a middle child with a sweet voice, unused to being the center of attention. She opens her mouth to sing.

I had a little nut tree
Nothing would it bear
But a silver nutmeg
And a golden pear.

This is who Minna sees, the little girl she carries in the present tense of her memory, eighty years later. She remembers my mother singing the second verse, too.

The King of Spain's daughter
Came to visit me
And all for the sake
Of my little nut tree.

I finish the coffee and turn off the hall light. I have managed not to wake them. Tomorrow, the King of Spain's daughter is leaving.

In the morning, I ask my father if he would fry me an egg for breakfast. His eggs are always delicious. When he sets the plate down in front of me, he is smiling, love in his eyes and pleasure at being able. 'I don't know, Dad; no one can make an egg like yours.' It's true. I try to duplicate his eggs at home, but even though I use his low-heat, slow-cooking method, my eggs never come out like his, crisp at the very edges, with the yolks intact.

The call comes. Massive stroke. Hit head when falling. Gash, blood all over mother's arm. 911. Ambulance. Intensive care. Drilling into his skull to relieve blood. The doctor who has treated my father for decades knows the seriousness of the situation. 'Call your daughter. Tell her to come.'

Still half-asleep, I roll over in bed and say to Steve, 'It's time.'

Two hours later I'm on a plane.

He lies peacefully, breathing deeply through a respirator. His ribs expand; his chest rises and falls. My mother and I stand at his bedside. She says the doctor has asked her, 'How far should we go to save him?' She has replied, 'Let him go.'

The doctor comes in. 'We're quite certain there's no more brain function. We can do a test to be certain, but I can already tell you the outcome.'

'No more tests,' my mother says, and I agree. The next step is clear: take him off the respirator and wait until he dies.

The tube is removed. His chest falls and barely rises. His ribs collapse. And yet I hear him continuing to breathe with loud strong breaths. At the side of his bed, the respirator is inhaling and exhaling on its own. I am about to ask the technician to shut off this last overlooked machine when the nurse who has been monitoring his functions tells us it's over.

My mother kisses his head. To him she says, 'I've loved you with all my heart and I will love you for the rest of my life. Goodbye, my boy. Sleep well.'

Now I am alone with him. I pass my hand over the fuzz on his bald head. I bend to his ear and whisper,

FUNEM?

S, VFM.

FUNEX?

S, VFX.

OK, MNX.

My father would jot down these letters and then swivel the piece of paper around to an unsuspecting guest, asking with delight, 'Can you read this?'

I was in on the secret. *Have you any ham? Yes, we have ham. Have you any eggs? Yes, we have eggs. Okay, ham and eggs.*

Mrs. Caggiano has sent a wreath. Platters of cold cuts have been ordered. I stay up late writing, deliver his eulogy dry-eyed:

One of the ways my father showed his affection was with a big hug. When you pulled back after that hug and looked at him, his smiling blue eyes would still be holding you.

Ellie wants to know how I was able to get through it without crying. The answer isn't hard. I've never been able to synchronize my feelings with the occasion. Things hit later. My mother's holding up the same way.

On the freeway going to CalArts, I get a panic attack. My colleagues are leading regular lives, but I am an outsider. My hands are on the wheel; any second I could lift them off. Luckily, I've got Patsy Cline on the tape deck. Breathe deep; sing along with Patsy.

One day I bend down to pick up a bag of dog food and can't straighten up. For days I lie in bed. The pain makes me whimper, which is what I want to do. I dream of a bottle tipping over, my father on his knees in a pool of black ink, his hands over his face, weeping.

I needed his signature on a scholarship application. He was sitting in the big armchair where he spent most of his time since he'd lost the grocery store. I brought him a bottle of black ink, a fountain pen, and the application form. He got up and looked around for a flat surface. Nearby was a drop-leaf table. The leaf had been raised, but it wasn't steady enough to take any weight, not even a hand writing a name.

'Please don't put it there,' I pleaded, but he didn't pay any attention to me.

He started to sign. His hand slipped, the leaf collapsed, the inkwell tipped, and black ink spilled over the application, onto the rug. I cried out, 'How could you do this to me?'

My father fell to his knees and dropped his head into his hands, crying again and again, 'I can't do anything right, I can't do anything right.'

When I got better, I went to a revival of *Carousel*. Billy Bigelow, the carnival barker, lies dying. Julie, who loves him, takes the shawl from her shoulders and covers his body. She bends over him and whispers, 'Sleep, my boy.'

On the way home I drive through the Sepulveda Pass, over the rise at Mulholland. The city below is lit up for the night. 'My father died,' I say and weep at last, all the way down into the Valley.

S everal months after my father's death, I was out with Byron on
the hillside behind our house. Ever the gentleman, Byron was
keeping me company, occasionally lifting his head to woof at a but-
terfly. I was sitting on a broken-off limb almost as big as a trunk. I
had the strangest sensation: the limb under me seemed to be breathing, each inhalation and exhalation carrying me ever so slightly but
unmistakably up and down and up again. I immediately thought that
this was my imagination, so I became logical, empirical. Was it real?
Not real?

Still in the same sitting position, I put my weight on my feet and
observed whether the limb was rising and falling under me. It was;
my weight could be discounted as the reason for the phenomenon.

I tried to lift the limb – perhaps it was lighter than it looked and
therefore susceptible to the current of a breeze. I couldn't begin to
budge it.

I sat on the limb with my full weight and carefully watched a particular piece of landscape against which I could measure the risings and fallings to see if my vision were affected.

Perhaps it was all in my mind, but no, while I felt myself being ever so slightly lifted and lowered, I calibrated the movement against a tree trunk in the middle distance. My eyes registered a minute but undeniable shift.

A week later, at the same time of day and in comparable weather, I conducted an experiment. I sat on that same limb for a while, purposely reading a book long enough to fool myself, almost, into forgetting my plan.

I looked up. The limb was still. Something had passed through and gone away.

3   *Limb.* In science: from the Latin, *limbe*,
meaning boundary, border

Everything that is interesting in nature
happens at the boundaries: the surface of the
earth, the membrane of a cell, the moment of
catastrophe, the start and finish of a life.

Nicholas Humphrey, *A History of Mind*

I never talk to anyone every day except my husband, so when I pledge to call my mother daily from California, this is not an easy thing. Five o'clock is good; it's the end of my day and for her it breaks up the evening.

We don't talk much about my dad. We mostly stay in the present as we adjust to a different world, ruled no longer by parents but populated instead by women.

Her main topic is how alone she is; no one ever calls or comes over.

'Who have you heard from lately?'

'No one.'

'No one?'

'Sylvia called the other day; her niece is moving to Minneapolis. Didn't you tell me it's a nice city?'

'Have you seen her recently?'

'No, she's much too busy. She goes out all the time with women of her own type, doctors' wives with plenty of money. She went to the opera last night; she has a subscription. I'm sure she looked beautiful. She phones me every morning, just to see if I'm all right, but I'm lucky if I get to see her once in two weeks. She's my bank, you know. She asks me how much I need. I write out a check, and she gives me cash.'

I swallow down the urge to point out Sylvia's devotion. I've learned that if I contradict her view, I become another one who doesn't understand.

'What's the latest with Dorothy? Is she still living in that big house of hers?'

'They'll have to carry her out of there. She's such a nut about that house, she can drive you crazy.'

'Is she still teaching?'

'She'll never stop. Her students have been taking classes with her for forty years; they can barely walk but they adore her.'

'Is she still painting?'

'I don't know where she gets the energy. She's a very lucky woman.'

I refrain from pointing out that Dorothy's husband died in middle age, that her daughter has cut off contact with her. That Dorothy has cultivated her gift. Lucky?

I phone to tell her she'd love the new Impressionist galleries at the Metropolitan Museum. When I walked through them the week before in New York, I felt almost as though I were swooning as the cool milky light poured from the skylights. I go on about the palette of colors on the gallery walls, the feeling of being in Europe. 'You must get better so that you can come to New York and see this.'

My zest falls flat. Her tone is chastising.

'Oh, no, no, no, that's over. I'm in such pain I can barely take a step in the house.'

Why couldn't she just say, 'It sounds so beautiful. Maybe we'll go someday, who knows?'

Petty . . . self-pitying . . . I get so furious. Recently I unearthed my birth certificate. In the box for Occupation of Parent, she had written 'Electrical engineer.' When I was born, my father was working at the Boston Naval Yard, part of the war effort. He replaced electrical cable on ships, but he was never an engineer. My birth certificate had been used for a passport.

Then she'll tell me a story that makes me realize her other qualities. She had a friend in the building, a woman she always talked about as someone special, 'above' her. Elsie had a college degree in social work, an unusual achievement for working-class Jewish girls of her time. The friendship was a matter of pride to my mother.

But people fail. In her later years, Elsie became obsessed with buying meat. She'd go to the market and buy big cuts of strip steaks, legs of lamb, roast beef, hunks of brisket. When there was no more room in her freezer, she asked her neighbors if they would keep her meat in their freezers.

A few weeks after Elsie died, my mother began to get phone calls. 'We've got Elsie's chops here; what should we do with them?' 'I've got her steaks; what do you think, should I defrost them?' Wisely, she suggested they phone Elsie's daughter.

To me, she said that the daughter should tell everyone to keep the meat and enjoy it.

'You know who sent me a photograph the other day? Kikuko, from Korea – you remember; she lived down the hall when her husband was interning at Mass General? You should see her sons; they're getting quite grown up.'

My mother had taught Kikuko to read English using my old children's books. After the family moved back to Korea, Kikuko sent my mother a card with calligraphy she had done herself, inscribing a quote from The Door in the Wall: FOLLOW THE WALL FAR ENOUGH AND THERE WILL BE A DOOR IN IT. This too will go into my eyeglass case. It's a little long, but I'll fold it in two.

Last night it was so nice to come home and find my mother's voice on the answering machine, wanting to know how I was feeling. She sounded strong, young, cleared of pain.

So many times when I'd venture to mention a physical problem, I'd hear, 'You had us so worried,' a remark that boomeranged off me and back to her own concern. This time, hearing her voice strong and sweet, the message genuinely inquiring, I felt comforted.

She has been left some money by a great-aunt, more than she has ever had in her life. Twelve thousand dollars. She's an heiress, at last. She tells me she wants to use some of the money to refurbish a rose velvet sofa she has lovingly tended through the years. She wants to know whether one day I'll want the sofa for my own house. I sense that only my assent will justify costly repairs to the frame, so I say yes, knowing that otherwise she'd wilt, her excitement undercut by realizing that her outlay would be for herself alone.

This is a crazy thing I'm doing, holed up at my word processor in California in order to see what I can recall of my parents' apartment. The furniture isn't even my taste, although I can hear myself in the future arguing with Steve as he voices his dislike for it while I put up a rear-guard argument in defense of what I've been told is 'good.'

I'm scanning the living room from the vantage point of my mother's wing chair. That bisque lamp of the shepherdess on the round table is to go to Ellie, who has long admired it. I've always thought it dreadful.

But now I remember the blush of pink on the shepherdess's cheek as she cradles a lamb in one arm, a basket filled with sheaves of corn at her feet. Each toe is beautifully articulated; there's a breath of suspirant life in this bisque. How can I ever part with it? I imagine my own house one day filled with objects I cannot bear giving up and cannot bear having around.

She already has given away a few things without asking me whether I wanted them.

'I'm your only child, aren't I?'

'I never thought you'd want my things.'

A Renoir reproduction in a gilded frame. An odd number of Limoges salad plates. A painting, done by Dorothy, of laundry blowing on a clothesline. Yes, I want it all.

My eye moves around the room like a camera, searching my memory for what comes next. Framed by a green cornice and drapes, the window sill holds a row of fine old glass vases, most of which I happen to know are cracked or chipped. She has turned them to the wall so no one will know.

A majestic table anchors the wall, a Wedgewood plate on its inlaid top. A side chair, its seat taut with ivory silk, stands between table and door, not to be used, really, but filling in space, like a nervously told anecdote.

What, on her request, will I eventually be called upon to give away to relatives and friends? What will I want to keep? I try to memorize which pieces she wants given to whom. I must ask her to write these things down.

What to save? What to discard? What to give away? The world accretes much as my parents have done, and future generations, sons and daughters all, may not know how to cope with all the things that are piling up, or falling apart, or disappearing. I'm going to try looking at this question as though it were one of DNA: what must I keep in order to preserve the genetic inheritance? The generation of my parents is becoming endangered; at the very least the stuff of their lives must be added to their children's genomes.

I've asked Minna to mail me newsletters from The Friendly Forum, her women's club from the old Dorchester neighborhood. The Friendly Forum lasted so long that some of the daughters eventually became members.

1943

It's been a long time, girls, but here is the same old excuse, due to war conditions, etc. we will have to be forgiven. However the ink is off the shelf, the paper is in the machine and the machine is in operation, so let's hope this edition meets with your approval.

HELPFUL FACTS
Two chocolate mints will offset the good of a brisk mile walk. One cinnamon bun just about balances an hour at the washboard.

IS IT TRUE OR FALSE?
A certain very honored member of the Friendly Forum is looking forward very eagerly to a vacation at Nantasket Beach? After theatening to shoot herself, we do hope Dora survives and has a very pleasant summer.

KIND ADVICE

Will someone please tell Rose to stop playing with the lock of her bag. It is very annoying.

REPORTED:

A Chicago woman, asked in a Red Cross questionnaire what had been her experience in the field of nutrition, wrote, 'I have been eating for years!'

IS IT TRUE OR FALSE THAT

A certain anxious mother of our group impersonated her charming daughter and tried to help her get a position? The mother, of course, gave her daughter quite a build up. We hope she got the job, Gert.

I hope Gert's daughter told her to lay off.

I'm continuing my tutorials, irritating everyone I know by insisting on seeing everything in terms of neurology.

'When I'm trying to recall my parents' living room, I feel as though I'm searching for an image that already exists in me.'

'It may feel that way,' says Dr. Fisher, 'but there's no place in your brain where the living room exists, no permanently held picture of a sofa. Very little is stored in the brain. For one thing, there wouldn't be enough room.

'Instead, think of your memories as connections constantly being made and unmade among synapses. The living room is delivered to you only during the window of time when you're reconstructing it.'

I'm opening that window. Francie, my mother's youngest sister, is sitting on the sand. She's in a two-piece bathing suit, a big smile on her face. I'm in her lap, little fists hugging each other in delight.

Francie on vacation with rich sister Jen. They're probably in Florida; miniature palms line the grounds of what looks to be a grand hotel. They're both wearing smart resort clothes, dresses with hemlines that look as though they'd flutter in the tropical breeze, platform shoes with ankle straps. Jen's hair unfurls off her face like stiff sails.

Leaning against a railing, the ocean behind her, Francie is in shorts that show off passably good legs; her midriff is bare. She has a glass of something in her hand, the way people do in advertisements when they're having fun.

Jen sits alone in the back seat of our car, on our way to see Francie. She tamps a cigarette on a gold mesh case and leans forward.

'Would you mind closing the window, Lou? It's making me cough.'

'No problem, Jen.'

He doesn't say a word about her emphysema. Everyone knows if Jen wants to do something, nothing anyone says will stop her.

My parents exchange glances as she flicks her lighter.

Sometimes a memory stops, holds itself in place. At those moments, the memory appears domesticated, as though it were being projected against the flapping screen of yesterday's laundry. Only briefly, though. Memory moves on as the sheets are reeled in.

The door is open to Francie and Jen's apartment; voices are coming from another room. I go down a corridor; to my right is the bathroom. That door is open too. White tiles. Red splashes.

We're walking through a hospital ward where patients are talking to themselves or standing motionless. I'm holding my mother's hand, trying to look straight ahead.

Francie sits at the edge of a bed in a private room paid for by Jen. Her head is down; she seems to be looking at the floor. My mother leads me up to kiss her. As she turns away, my lips graze her cheek.

I've borrowed a book from the library, *The History of Psychosurgery* by Eliot Valenstein. The book has sat on my desk for over a month now. It would be a lot easier to give it back. But I won't. I've made a pledge to myself that I'll read it all the way through.

I'm forcing myself to copy down, word by word, a description of exactly what happens during a prefrontal lobotomy. Maybe if I use my own hands to type the words onto the page, I can get through it.

The brain was approached from the lateral surface of the skull . . . holes were drilled on both sides of the cranium, after which a 6-inch cannula, the tube from a heavy-gauge hypodermic needle, was inserted through one hole and aimed toward the hole on the opposite side of the head. . . .

When the cannula was withdrawn, a blunt spatula – much like a calibrated butter-knife – was inserted about 2 inches into the track left by the cannula. After the spatula was inserted, its handle was swung upward so that the blade could be drawn along the base of the skull, and a cut was made as far to the side as possible. The spatula was then withdrawn, and the site was rinsed. At length four quadrants were cut, two on each side of the brain, and the results varied, generally producing a pacifying effect.

There. It's copied. I did it.
But I don't feel very well.

'Minna, I've never understood why Francie had a lobotomy.'

'She's the one I feel awful about. She was depressed, and nothing the doctors tried brought her out of it. Don't forget, she saw things no child should see – the terrible fights between my mother and father, and of course all the violence around Herbie. She was the youngest, so she was alone with him after we had all left.

'She grew up to be a withdrawn person, but she could work. people liked her, Ellie adored her. Like most of us in those days, she got married. Two pathetic people met each other. But they were happy at first, and we all loved Harry. Then he was drafted and

Francie went out to join him at the army base in Reno. Harry started to gamble. He left Francie alone, night after night. She'd never been away from the family, and she felt abandoned. That's when she started to cry all the time.'

'Was it any better after they came back here, when she had all of you around?'

'Yes, at the beginning. They had a little apartment in Brighton. Francie used to say it was the happiest time of her life.

'Then Jen insisted they move in with her. Jen was older, she didn't have a family of her own, and she had earned a lot of money from her dress store. She wanted Francie to have a more comfortable life, she said, than Harry could provide. She kept giving Francie money and presents, things Francie didn't need or even want, but Jen used them to hold on to her.

'Francie knew it wasn't right for her, but she wasn't strong enough to say no. She turned to me. She pleaded, "Minna, save me." But I was afraid. I had my own family, my own life. I didn't want to do anything to rock the boat.

'Harry felt under Jen's thumb and walked out on Francie. That was the blow that did it. Nothing we did helped, not all the psychiatrists, not the electric shock treatments. She would weep and weep.

'After Harry left, Francie tried to kill herself, not once but many times. The doctors said she should have a minimal lobotomy, something they were doing in those days. They said it would stop the suicide attempts.'

Francie and Herbie sit at a nightclub with the rest of the family. He is wearing a bow tie and is expressionless other than the slight downturn of his lips. Her hair has been sprayed into a bubble; she too is without expression, slumped down into her chair. They look like zombies.

Was it just that one evening, that one photograph? Please, let it be. But no, from then on this is how Francie and Herbie always appear, in the midst of some family gathering where everyone else is smiling at the camera. This is how I remember them, deadened and claimed.

They were cared for; they remained in the family fold. But it was the family that did this to them.

The neurologists reported that Madame I was incapable of normal recall. Although she could generate momentary images, she had lost the ability to connect them into a continuous memory. Nor could she create an ongoing sense of the present.

Physical examination revealed that while Madame I had normal sensitivity to touch, she was completely insensitive to pain. Denys and Camus speculated that Madame I had lost the link between her body and her self.

Madame I lived in Paris at the turn of the century, Francie in Boston at the century's midpoint: both women lived with incessant weeping. Perhaps by living without continuous feeling, Madame I was staunching a deeper grief. Impervious to sensation, was she protecting herself against pain greater than she could bear?

'Minna, I saw the bathroom when Francie tried to kill herself. You were all so involved with Francie, no one realized I was there. There was blood all over the tiles.'

'We never should have let you see that, you were just a dear little girl who walked into something awful.'

'It wasn't that bad. To be honest, it wasn't nearly as awful as when my dog died around that same time.'

'Please,' Minna says. 'Forgive us.'

'Excuse me . . . excuse me,' I call out, trying to get the attention of the woman I spotted in the rearview mirror on the way to meet Ellie.

I run to catch up with her. 'I hope you don't mind my asking but . . .'

She swings around, pivoting on a crutch. I'm surprised; from the back, I'd imagined her older, not a handsome woman in her forties who, with an inquiring tilt of her blond head, seems open to my question.

'. . . did you have a problem afterward with phantom pain? My mother lost her leg and . . .'

With a thick accent, she says that she has only just come to this country six months ago. Her operation was done in Russia, where, she claims, they do it so well that people don't suffer. She has heard that in America, surgeons cut the nerves badly. 'I hear it can be excruciating,' she says with the commiserative air of the fortunate. As she pivots away, she wishes my mother good luck.

I surprised myself with my brashness, running after a stranger to ask such a personal question, but my mother's situation has become extreme. New tests have revealed a serious blockage in the so-called good leg. Dr. MacKenzie, her surgeon, advises another bypass. She's dead set against it.

He says, 'The vast majority need five, six, seven days in the hospital; it's not that much of a deal. Look, this isn't God's work; it's human engineering.'

He did add that some surgeries are more difficult than others, and indeed, the incision will be groin to ankle. He says my mother can expect to have 'local pain for two or three weeks on the way to healing.'

This is the doctor who said that virtually none of his patients ever experienced phantom limb. He's either living in a dream world or a believer that a stiff upper lip produces better results. Nuts! I want a true assessment, even if it errs too far in the direction of predicting pain.

When my mother continues to refuse, he says, 'All we can do is hope she'll be lucky this time. If she lives very quietly and does nothing to disturb the leg, she might be okay.'

Shall I tell her how limited her choices really are?

'Have you noticed how many little details you have to deal with all the time?' asks Ellie when we meet for coffee. She's her usual self, handbag and shoes matching, but the strain shows around her eyes and she has gained a few pounds.

'It's no fun. Do you know what I do when I leave my parents' apartment? You must never say another word about this, but I get into my car, roll up all the windows, and I scream.'

All over America, adults are screaming. I hear them in small towns in Maine, in front of doormen buildings on Park Avenue, and along the Wilshire Corridor of Los Angeles, screaming in sealed cars in border towns in Texas, in the driveways of two-family homes in Wisconsin, in Boston and La Crescenta. I hear America screaming, its grown children trying not to be heard.

At my mother's request, I've brought tweezers to the hospital where she's recovering from this last round of tests. Until now, I never knew that, left unchecked, my mother would have several long hairs sprouting from her upper lip and chin. She has asked whether I could pluck them.

'My own mother asked me to do this,' she says, 'when she was in the hospital, but I didn't have time right then and there, so I told her I'd do it a little later. She died that day, before I got back. I always felt awful that I'd failed to do that one little thing for her.'

I surprise myself; I like doing it. The tweezers have a slant edge, not ideal for leaning over the bed and getting a firm grasp on the base of each hair. But little by little, I do the job, shifting from one side of the bed to the other like an expert. When I'm done, I tilt the mirror up to her face. It's good, she says.

. I'm about to leave for the airport when a fire alarm rings. A nurse runs along the corridor slamming doors shut. On the public address system there's an announcement: no one can leave the building until the all-clear. I'm trapped in my mother's room with an empty bed on the other side of her.

I'd been in the hospital for several days. A week earlier, I'd delivered the final blow to an already sprained neck when I sat with my then-boyfriend, two cinephiles in our twenties, devotedly looking up from the second row for the three hours of a French nouvelle vague film.

I unhooked myself from traction and went over to the window that overlooked a drained swimming pool in Mount Morris Park. The walls of the pool had been painted a sharp aqua; around the pool was a screen of trees with dusty-looking yellow leaves. I was getting to know this view well: it's what I saw at night when the pinched nerve in my arm woke me, needing cradling like a prickly baby.

My mother phoned. 'How's your new roommate?'

'That's a whole story,' reluctant to talk in front of the woman in the other bed, even though she was deaf.

'Young or old?'
'Old.'
'Alone?'
'I think so.'
'Poor thing.'

'Where's my purse? They took it from me at the desk. They never asked me to sign for it. I had to give them my ring, Where's my ring? I never go out without it. . . .'

ASK THE NURSE!

I nodded in the direction of the door and then emphatically at Miss Goldstein: IT'S BEEN THREE DAYS, TELL HER TO GET YOUR RING FOR YOU.

But she was afraid to ask.

Outside in the corridor, I heard the residents conferring about Miss. G.'s case. A deep voice, the young Hawaiian doctor? ' . . . severe ulcerated varicosity. I've been following the case since August.' They trooped in, a cohort of young men surrounding Miss G.'s bed.

I didn't want to give away my concern for fear they'd lower their voices, so I concentrated on a pitcher of orange berries, a present from my friend JoAnn, who knew I'd missed autumn this year.

'Berries,' Miss G. had joined in, 'I had those too. A girlfriend from the office, they grew in her backyard. She used to bring them in for me.' From the corner of my eye, I glimpsed them unwrapping Miss G.'s bandages.

Miss Wagner burst in.

'They found your ring!' she shouted.

Miss G. looked up, puzzled, squinting to hear.

'THEY'VE FOUND YOUR RING!'

I couldn't contain myself. 'Wonderful!'

Through the encircling doctors, I saw Miss G. rise up in bed and grasp Miss Wagner's hand.

'They found it?'

Miss Wagner nodded. 'Yes, yes, here's your bag, you see? That nurse at the desk was honest after all!'

The young doctors bent over her. She didn't cry out as they passed their instruments back and forth, lancing away tissue. They trooped out.

Miss G. raised herself on her elbows.

'See what they did to me?'

She pointed to her legs, criss-crossed with adhesive strapping.

She was quiet.

Then she held out her left hand and looked at it, pointing it in my direction, her fourth finger extended. 'My brother, he used to be a jeweler. He made it, for my mother. She left it to me.'

I walked over to her bedside and touched the narrow gold band. I turned it slightly, her hand turning with mine, palm upward to show me the ring's filigree. I admired it and said nothing about what I noticed first of all – the setting lacked a stone. There were a few prongs, but they surrounded a small hollow.

The night before I was discharged, I stood at the window once more, but not because of pain. I looked down at the drained pool, at the browning trees, and wondered what happens to a tree if its leaves don't turn color before they fall.

The owner of a bed and breakfast in Taos looks at Steve and me strangely and replays messages she'd found that morning on her answering machine.

'I think my daughter is dead. Can you please phone me?'

A second message. This time my mother is crying.

'My daughter is dead; I know it, but no one will return my call.'

Later that morning there's another message.

'This is your cousin Ellie. Your mother has gone crazy. She's certain you died in an automobile accident. Are you all right?'

We'd been looking forward to this vacation in New Mexico, but after I exchange calls with her doctor, it's inevitable, I have to go back to Boston.

I call my mother and tell her I'm coming.

'No,' she says. 'Stay where you are. When your vacation is over, you'll come to Boston and I can die. Have a good time. At least I'll have accomplished that.'

Have a good time?

She folds and unfolds a piece of paper. She opens and shuts her purse. Again and again and again. She's certain she's penniless: 'I'm in trouble,' she whispers, as though afraid of being overheard by creditors. Nothing I say reassures her. She says my father is asking her to join him.

I race around Boston on automatic, making necessary arrangements, going from bank to bank closing accounts where my father had squirreled away little bits of money, opening a new account in my name so that I'll be able to handle her finances from afar.

Then I drive out to Roslindale to pick up an application to the Hebrew Center for the Aging, where there's always a long waiting list.

'This is not about your going into the Home,' I say. 'It's only an insurance policy. When your name comes up we can always say no.'

Her hand is so unsteady her signature wavers up and down the application. I'm tremulous too, but I can cover it up.

Little by little over the next few weeks, her mind clears until she's fully herself again. I would happily walk on my knees to give thanks, that's how grateful I am.

'Drug-induced dementia,' says the eminent pain specialist who had put her on synthetic morphine for the phantom limb pain. She says she'll never go back to him. The idea of adjusting dosages is out of the question. No more painkillers.

But an idea has been raised. Every day now I think about it: does she need more care than home health can give? One person takes care of her, and if she can't come, there's a back-up person. But the system doesn't always work; several times she has faced the prospect of spending the night alone. Without help, she's unable to fend for herself. At night she can pivot off the bed and onto the commode right beside her; during the day, once she has been settled into a wheelchair, she can get herself into the bathroom, stand on one leg, and, using raised bars, swing herself over to the toilet. I happen to know that she often falls; she won't tell me, but the aides do. If she were alone in the house, she wouldn't be able to get up.

Meanwhile the 'good' leg is getting worse; it needs to be carefully watched. At the Home, she'd have a nursing staff, people all around her . . .

Then I hear her say she's happy to do nothing all day, just sit and look at the apartment, that's how much pleasure it gives her. She fought for that apartment, getting on the waiting list as soon as she heard about a luxury building with subsidized units for low-income families. When an apartment came through, she cautioned me about keeping up appearances: 'No one must know.' If anyone in the building asked what my father did for a living, I was to answer, 'He's in transportation.'

Then there's that other question: can we go on paying for her home care? Yes and no. My father left me nothing. Well, to be fair, he left me thirteen thousand dollars which paid for less than ten weeks of her care. He used to go over his accounts with me, showing how he'd worked everything out, a certificate of deposit in one bank, another somewhere else, three different savings accounts plus the credit union. He was so proud; she'd be all right, no matter what happened to him. My mother would shake her head silently.

I suppose it might have worked. With subsidized rent, social security, a boost from us, she would have had enough. But she knew what I didn't. Things don't go that way. Something happens.

Once the money was used up, we assumed the costs for round-the-clock care. Steve has been wonderful; he takes it as a given – this is what we have to do. I'm continually astonished that I've grown up to be financially comfortable. I always assumed I'd be struggling just to get by. I'm grateful each time I fly to Boston on a moment's notice, aware of all the years I couldn't afford to do that. But money is draining from our savings.

I ask Minna what she thinks. 'Our lives are over. We've had our day. Nobody expects you to give up your life for hers.'

One hour I decide that the Home is the right course; the next hour my heart goes into reverse. I phone her old friend Sylvia to ask what she thinks.

'She needs more care than she's getting. But she's a woman of great dignity, and it's being stripped from her.'

'What's the point of living this way?' my mother asks me, speaking about her unappeasable pain.

'If you need any help, any kind whatsoever' – verbally underlining 'whatsoever,' in case she's serious about not wanting to live – 'you know I'm here for you.'

'Help? What kind of help can you give me?'

'What kind of help? Here I am thinking about her needs, sacrificing my own – she just doesn't get it.'

'She knows what you do for her, believe me,' Minna says.

'Then why does she make me feel that nothing I do makes a difference?'

'Pain makes people different from the way they really are. It's hard on you, but bear with her.'

Minna puts the force of her thin body into the word 'bear,' letting it travel down on the current of her exhale, bringing relief to me.

By now we've talked about it so many times that we both seem to be accepting the necessity. But then she asks for a stay. She can't face it.

The important thing now is to get her assigned to the right building in the Home, the one where people are able to function with some independence and are more or less mentally intact. She's terrified that she'll have to go to the other building, where Herbie lived after my grandmother's death, the place for people who need more vigilant attention. My mother could be assigned there only because she needs so much help with the basics. I agree: it's out of the question.

It was in the residents' dining room that Herbie died, choking on a peanut. At the time I distanced myself from his death, choosing to think of it as theater of the absurd. Now I know that decades after a lobotomy, a person can lose the will to swallow.

She practices. When I get to Boston, she calls me to come from the living room to the doorway of her bedroom. There she is, her hands on the armrests of her wheelchair, slowly pushing herself up. Then she lifts her hands off the supports and grasps the walker. Wearing her leg, she is upright again, the first time in many months.

'Great! You did it!' I cheer.

She smiles, looking up like a shy and proud little girl. She takes a step, and then another. By the day of the interview, she thinks she can use the leg with a walker for a few hours. When we arrive at the Home, both of us tastefully dressed, we give the right impression: lovely cultured people, my mother gracious and able to fend for herself. Sarah, the admitting social worker, is taken with her; I tell her about my mother's good eye for interior design, and the three of us cook up a scenario in which my mother will advise the gift shop on how best to arrange its items. Actually, it's the two of us, Sarah and myself; although my mother goes along, she's too aware of her physical limitations. But for today, she even manages to go to the ladies room by herself, while I try to cover up my nervousness. Hurray – she makes it back! I'm so proud of her.

Sarah agrees; she deserves a shot at the good building. After all the paperwork is complete, we should give her a sign, she says, that we're ready, and my mother's name will be moved up on the waiting list. 'But,' she says, 'I don't want to promise you anything. We never know when a bed will come up, so you may not get a roommate who is as intact as you are.'

The Friendly Forum

KEEPING BUSY IS AN ANTIDOTE TO FEAR

Should an air raid come, keeping busy reduces one's fear of it. Plan in advance how you will spend your time even if in darkness. Maintain your normal everyday interests and activities as much as possible, and you will find yourself thinking very little of the civilian hazards of war. If you feel anxious, make yourself a center of security and reassurance for someone less sturdy than yourself. What the future holds for us we do not know. Of one thing we may be certain. We will be found adequate in all ways.

TRUE OR FALSE?

Yoo Hoo, Gert. Is it true that you've been parading around Blue Hill Avenue dressed up in red slacks?

RUMORS

It is rumored that those of us who did not summer in Nantasket were at a loss by not seeing Dora swim.

Speaking of Dora, she isn't the only one who can slap a man in the face for degrading the Jews. Leave it to Rose to go one better. She knocked a guy out and said, as a parting shot, 'Here, take this, you dirty dog, I wish I were a man. I'd do worse.' I wonder how much worse she could have done.

ORCHIDS

I think we should all take a bow and congratulate ourselves on raising such a large sum of money for the war effort in such a short period of time. May good fortune shine on all our enterprises as it did on this. A GREAT BIG ORCHID TO ALL OF US.

I'm so impressed with the guts, the mind, the heart of these women. Like Dora, like Rose. When it was time for Dora to go into a nursing home, Minna told me she walked out of her apartment and didn't look back. My mother did the same thing. They leave like gladiators, forward to face their fates. Their daughters close the doors behind them.

After a few puzzled glances, a woman two doors down recognizes my mother. It's Rose from The Friendly Forum, she of the nervous clasp and the strong arm. I'm enthusiastic; with a link to her past, my mother won't feel so cut off.

After Rose leaves, my mother says, 'I hope she doesn't want to talk too much about the old days.'

I start putting things away, putting bras and underpants in a top drawer where they'll be easy to reach, consulting with her about where to hang Dorothy's painting. It's small, just laundry on a clothesline, but there's a wind blowing through it.

Steve has come with me for a few days. My mother, sitting in her wheelchair surrounded by the confusion of belongings not yet put away, looks up at his tall form.

'That's a beautiful apple you're eating, very unusual, those red and gold markings.'

For years, Steve has lumped my mother and me together as two beauty nuts who turn to beauty as a way not to see ugliness. What he doesn't understand is that we can't help it; color hits us between the eyes, a stunned blow we have no choice but to acknowledge. I went to India wanting to see streets full of melon and orchid saris, to Iran to see Isfahan's blue. My mother hasn't had those opportunities, but an apple will do.

Steve has had to go back to California. Now all that's left in the apartment is the bed I'll sleep on this last time, a radio, and a lamp so that I can read myself to sleep. I'm proud of myself. I've managed to get every single thing – each dish – to a person she cares about. I'm bone weary.

I turn on the radio and get lucky with a great blues show featuring the irresistible Elmore James. I haul myself up and start to move with the music, into the den, then from room to empty room, taking bigger steps than I've ever been able to make in the apartment before.

I circle along the indentations in the rug where the dining room table had been, over to the place that used to be set for guests.

'Steve, here's where you sat when I brought you to meet my parents . . .'

I boogie into the bedroom, along a wall with holes made by picture hooks –

'Mum, here's where you hung that godawful picture of me.'

Into the kitchen stripped of its pots and pans, I'm calling, singing, stomping, circling.

'Daddy, here's where you made me an egg . . .'

I'm out of breath. I lean against the wall, breathing hard. I try to start up again, but it's over.

When I spot a woman who might be my mother's type, I strike up a conversation, 'That's a lovely color you're wearing. . . . Yes, this is my beloved mother. I'm pleased that you think we look alike; it's a compliment.' When we get out of the elevator, my mother asks me to stop trying to fix her up. 'I know you mean well, but I can manage by myself.'

Let's go out together, Dora, and wear our dresses. No, Helen, that is why I didn't come up from the beach to attend meetings this summer. After all, you spent less for your dress. I haven't got a sister who owns a dress shop, like Jen. But I can get other things wholesale. For instance, hats.

Later she tells me how much it means to hear me introduce her as my beloved mother. She says it thrills her. 'When you talk to people, you have such a sparkle in your eyes,' she says to me. 'I've fallen in love with you.'

And I with her. This is the grace of the last years, the children coming to understand the contradictions in their parents, not to reconcile them but encompass them in a larger love.

She wonders whether my lipstick color would look good on her. 'Here, try it.' I watch while she puts it on slowly, little dabbing strokes, looking intently into a hand mirror as if to avoid making a mistake.

'At least you have full lips,' she says, coloring a little outside her lip line. 'When you get old, they won't get so thin they'll almost disappear.

'I always hated having thin lips,' she goes on. 'When I was little – I couldn't have been more than ten or eleven – I had a girlfriend I was crazy about. She had a horrible mother who looked down on my family because her family had a successful dry goods store in Poland and they were able to bring over a little money with them. The mother had a big mouth, and if she didn't like you, she'd let you know in no uncertain terms. I was such a scared, insignificant thing; I used to jump if anyone said anything to me. That day I must have done something to irritate Mrs. Blindner because she got angry and turned to me: 'You have thin lips, that's why. That's what's wrong with you, thin lips.'

'The witch!'

For years, probably three-quarters of a century, my mother has thought her lips were ugly. Now I know why she has always put her lipstick on so tentatively, depositing a fuschia dab on a front tooth.

'I think you'd do better with a brighter color.'

'Your father never liked me to wear bright lipstick.'

With a short dinner dress, pin artificial flowers in your hair and swirl veiling around them. You'll be the center of every admiring glance.

I enjoy buying clothes for her, putting outfits together. When she opens a box, she gasps, smiles, then holds her hand to her mouth like a little girl given something beyond her ken. 'It's beautiful, much nicer than anything I'd buy for myself. But you're spending too much money on me. How much did this cost you?'

Scoop. Flash, The Sherman sisters are all sporting new plaid suits. Jen, Minna, and Francie better not go out together and also Helen better call up Pauline in Harrisburg before you decide to wear your new suit – who knows, someone could see you tho' far away.

4 And at the penultimate porches, the dark-red
mantle of the body's memories slips and is
absorbed . . .

D. H. Lawrence

In the end, I wasn't able to get rid of that heavy artificial leg she kept in the closet. I didn't know what to do with it, so I shipped it back along with everything else.

It's away from sight, but I keep seeing limbs. On the cover of a museum newsletter there's a photograph of a leg protruding from a white wall. I'm trying to figure out how the thing works. Did the artist cut a hole in the wall, lie on the other side, and stick his own leg through? Or did he arrange for someone else to lie on the floor while he framed the image in his camera? Between the end of the pant leg and the ribbed sock is a patch of skin with dark curly hair; a man probably, although it could be a woman. The pant leg ends midcalf; it looks as though a cylindrical limb had been pushed through it and out the other end, a tube within a tube like an old-fashioned ice cream pop.

You could push from the shoe side, and the leg would retract into the pant. Or go to the other side, insert your arm into the pant, and make the leg reemerge, like a hand puppet peering out into the world. The shoe could be made to rotate like Clark Gable's periscope in *Run Silent, Run Deep.*

Later I learn that the leg doesn't belong to anyone. All that time I'd been looking at a photograph of a sculpture.

What is it with a leg? Internal organs get removed all the time; nobody's happy about it, but they're not as horrified as if they'd had to lose an external part of themselves. Is it the spectre of helplessness? Is it the way we use legs as metaphors: in homage, we walk in another's footsteps. 'Isn't it time he stood on his own two feet?' Or maybe it's because standing on two legs is what defines us as human beings?

The earliest known footprints of an erect person have been discovered at Laetoli, in Africa. What if only one footprint had been discovered? Would anthropologists have known it for what it might well have been, the imprint of a woman who had lost a leg?

From wherever I am, I make my daily five o'clock phone calls to my mother's new number. The social worker has encouraged me to be in touch with her, too, about my mother's condition, but I seldom phone her because she has a tendency to dither. 'She's next to useless,' my mother says. To me, the social worker has said my mother's making a place for herself. My mother tells me she's miserable. It's hard to know from far away which, if any, truth prevails.

She makes history at the Home by becoming the first person ever to try its new acupuncture treatment. I'm surprised; then I remember she's on an antidepression medication that has opened her to possibility. She says the doctor was surprised by her. 'I guess he thought he was going to see a scared little old lady.'

Afterward, the staff praises her courage; even the head of the hospital drops by to give her a pat on the back.

I never thought she cared for reading, but she tells me she used to read all the time, holding a book in one hand while stirring my baby formula with the other. She'd get so absorbed, she says, she'd scorch the pan.

Her preference now is for Jewish family sagas that take place over generations, a finite genre she's close to exhausting. One day in my local bookstore, it hits me: those family stories are everywhere; it's just that they're being told by writers who aren't Jewish. I go on a book-buying binge, mailing her novels by Amy Tan, Louise Erdrich, Cristina Garcia. I have one proviso: that she tell me what she thinks of them. Some she likes, others not at all, but she's interested in most of them.

My mother tells me about a television program she'd seen about tigers, which my father would have enjoyed because he was crazy about tigers. I had no idea. I tell her that for my birthday, Steve and I are going to an ice dancing show, something I've always loved. My mother says my father liked watching ice skating on television.

Sylvia brings scones, which my mother has never tried. Minna bakes a bundt cake.

I send photos of the new curtains in our kitchen. Ellie brings a thermos for keeping tea hot at her bedside.

But it's clear, gifts cannot hold her in place.

One evening, a new doctor phones. The 'good' leg has begun to turn blue. There's nothing more they can do to save it.

She no longer offers her goodness as a weight against horror. She faces up to the nothingness, to the soon-to-be-empty space where something should be.

She will no longer have a footprint, no longer make a tread upon the earth.

With both legs gone, her center of gravity will shift. It is the foot that grounds us.

She will be virtually helpless.

She must not suffer phantom limb pain again. I fax Dr. Fisher – is there anything you know that might help? He sends back an article suggesting that an epidural administered right before an amputation might block the nerves' pathways.

Dr. MacKenzie is skeptical. He hasn't heard of this approach.

I tamp down my anger; we need him on our side.

When we speak a few days later, he claims he hasn't had time to read the article.

I press.

'You've known us for a long time. Please, I ask you, consider this.'

JoAnn, my old friend, has come up to Boston to be with me during the operation. I can't sit alone in that waiting room.

'There's a call for you.'

It's MacKenzie, saying my mother has got through the operation and is in the recovery room. Then he adds, 'I used the epidural. I don't know whether it will work.'

I'm feeling too triumphant for his disclaimer. This time, I swear, I'll defeat the pain of phantom limb.

She weighs sixty-five pounds, her nurse tells me. I gasp, 'So little? She weighed seventy-five pounds last week.' The nurse reminds me that now the other leg is gone.

'I'm going to need a child's size casket,' my mother cries.

The soundless O of her mouth.

Teeth clenched, fists waving.

Her agony is being seared into my brain. I don't want it. I haven't any choice.

Call Steve, call friends. Long distance. Hearing Steve's voice helps.

'I miss you. I went to a great restaurant the other night . . . I've been reading a good mystery . . . I saw the show, it wasn't all that good . . . Come back. I know you have to be there, but this is getting too hard.'

'I'm like an animal . . . put me to sleep.'

Three days later and she's still in pain worse than anything I've ever seen before.

I can't stand it.

I don't remember ever saying that before.

I'm so alone.

It's so cold. I come back to the hotel room chilled to the bone. I don't want to be in a hotel room, but there's no other place to stay.

I'm falling behind. I can't stay any longer.

I try to plan everything in advance, hire an aide to take care of her during the transfer back to the Home, ask Ellie if she'd ride in the ambulance with her as I had on the way there, talking a blue streak to divert her from nausea.

Now, though, everything's different. She is without legs.

Oh Mum.

I put my hand on her forehead and smooth away the ridges of our past griefs. My heart goes out to her, no barriers, and she knows it.

For years she has been saying, 'Go home to your husband, where you belong.' She has meant this in a nice way, to relieve me of my burdens, to say that she's all right and I shouldn't worry. I've been grateful. Today the words are beyond her, but I can see from the look in her green-brown eyes and the touch of her hand on my wrist that she means it.

And I go, knowing I shouldn't.

There's no phone in her room, so they've wheeled her out to the nurses' station. She's not up to conversation, so we talk just a tiny bit, enough for me to say 'I love you,' and her to say 'I love you' back. I say goodbye, and there's silence. It's clear she doesn't know what to do: she can't reach to put the phone receiver on its cradle. She holds on, waiting for someone to come, saying again and again, 'Goodbye.'

A few days later, at five in the morning, her doctor calls. My mother has a blood clot in her 'good leg,' now the name for the part of her leg that remains from the first amputation. She has slipped into a coma. It's possible to try to save her, but it would mean sending her back in an ambulance where she'd undergo a surgical procedure to locate the exact location of the clot, which might indicate that the leg would have to be amputated higher up.

Or we can put her on a morphine drip. She won't have any pain; she'll slip deeper into the coma and die. What do I want to do?

Let her go. Her agony must stop.

Before I call the doctor back, I phone Minna to make certain she agrees. In the firm voice she can call up in a crisis, she says, 'Let her go.'

Then I call Ellie to make sure my mother won't be alone until I get there. Steve is on the other line calling airlines, trying to get us on the next plane out.

'All she needs is people with her,' I say, hoping Ellie will get there as fast as she can.

'That's all she's been needing – oh, I shouldn't have said that.'

'What did you mean?'

'Nothing.'

'Say it!'

'For the last few days your mother has been calling for you.'

'Why didn't anyone call me?'

'We thought you were too busy – '

Too busy?

I hang up on her.

Steve runs in. 'Why are you screaming?'

'My mother's going to die without me.'

I'm walking fast from room to room, doubled over.

'What did I do wrong?'

Steve tries to hold me. 'You didn't do anything wrong.'

'I should have been there.'

I got to Boston in time to see her eyes, which had slipped to one side, focus again on me as I held her head in my palm. To this day, I carry the weight of her head in my palm, her silky gray hair, her eyes trying to find me. I said a word I didn't know I had in me, a word she called me when I was growing up, in Yiddish, which she herself didn't speak.

'Fagelah,' I said. 'My little bird.'

'With your toe, go tap tap tap, with your hand go clap clap clap . . .' In a circle, I put my foot in the center and tap three times. My mother is in the circle too, leading and singing. Then she is mounting the podium, speaking in a firm sweet voice as the lights of the Garden go down.

At the funeral home, the director greets me warmly. 'I liked your parents so much. I miss your father. Do you know that he used to drop in when he was in the neighborhood? Being in a funeral home makes a lot of people uneasy, but not your dad. He'd stick his head into my office and say, "Hi, Babs, got a minute to shoot the breeze?" And he loved your mother so much, right up to the end. Would you like to see her?'

I expect to traipse through a long corridor, but she leads Steve and me around the corner.

'Would you like to be alone with her?' she asks.

Steve and I stand there, shocked that my dead mother was on the other side of the wall all the time we were talking with the funeral director. Death has changed her profile, making her more severe, her cheek more hollow, her cheekbone higher. 'She looks like Abraham Lincoln,' I whisper to Steve, and he agrees. Death strips. Not like her profile when she took off the wig. No, something far more final. No more change is possible.

A sharp wind blows under the canopy. Minna is helped up the grassy slope by Ellie holding her by the elbow. Sylvia looks pinched under a fur coat. Dorothy looks artificially vivid, her jet black hair surrounding an old sorrowful face.

My parents made arrangements for themselves long ago, the plots bought, the coffins chosen, everything paid for and kept up. Near the end, my mother specified a change: she wanted a graveside service, no long cortege from the funeral home to the cemetery.

'Are you sure, Mum? You're not doing this to save money, are you? Because that would be silly.'

She said it's what she wants.

Earlier I'd spoken with the rabbi, someone recommended by a friend of Ellie's. I tried to give him a sense of her, but when he speaks at the service, he gets it wrong. He talks so much about her love of beautiful things that she sounds like the person she wanted to be, a collector of fine china, an affluent operagoer. He has diminished her real triumphs.

I don't cry this time either, not when well-wishers come up and embrace me, not during the service when I read a favorite poem of my mother's.

How do I love thee? Let me count the ways . . .
I love thee with a passion put to use
In my old griefs, and with my childhood's faith.

. . . and, if God choose,
I shall but love thee better after death.

I weep only when I'm hugged by a cousin from my father's side of the family. He and I had never meant much to each other, but now he takes my tears as evidence of a greater closeness. But that isn't it. I'm crying because there's nothing left to hold us together.

At Ellie's house I try to act on Steve's advice: 'You can afford to be the bigger one. Make up with her. After all, she's family.' I give her a hug, but she doesn't yield. I can just hear it: 'Should we call her?' 'No, let's wait and see what happens. She has other things to do.'

Cold cuts. Chit-chat. At the end, Sylvia leaves without saying goodbye to me.

Before we go back to California, Steve and I drop in to see Minna, who complains about how freezing cold she was at my mother's funeral. She wants to know why I decided to have it on a day when it was so cold. I explain about the prediction for snow the following day.

Then she questions my choice of a graveside funeral.

'Everyone was freezing. It would have been so much better in the chapel. I hate to say it, but I had to pee so badly from standing out in the cold that I couldn't think about anything else, and in the end I couldn't hold it in.'

I tell her that I was carrying out my mother's instructions, that she had been adamant about it.

Her tone disbelieving that I could know something about my mother that she didn't know, Minna says, 'I never thought she wanted a graveside funeral. She never said anything about it to me.'

I am walking along Harvard Street, between Commonwealth Avenue and Beacon Street. I am walking fast, the way a very cold person does. The way a very angry person does.

I've come from a chiropractor who knows how to undo the knots my body gets into when I'm in Boston. Goodbye, Dr. Katz, I won't need your services anymore.

Goodbye to it all, goodbye to Wolf's where we had a sandwich after Daddy died. Goodbye to the fish market where they have the best-quality fish that my parents bought only when I was coming home.

Goodbye to the tailor who took in my mother's clothes. Should I go in and tell her? No.

Goodbye to Cherry & Webb where she bought cheap clothes that looked expensive. Goodbye to Pik-a-Chik, to the Chinese restaurant, to the knitting store, to the man who fixes lamps, to the cafe where I'd meet Ellie.

Goodbye to the Eagle Deli, where my father was a regular. Goodbye to Ellie, to Angela, yes, even to Minna. I won't be coming back.

She comes back to me in all sorts of ways. I'm driving, and I hear her voice asking me to call when I get home, just to say I've arrived safely. No one is looking out for me. Not in that way.

In a doctor's office, I have to fill out a form. 'Next of kin.' What should I write in that space?

Relief. No five-o'clock bell going off in my head, 'time to call her,' and if I put it off, no voice saying 'She must be worried, I'd better call first thing in the morning.' I'm free. Time for myself now.

A world is gone. No Sylvia, no Dorothy. No doctors. No home health aides. No social security forms to fill out, no bank statements to keep track of. No social workers. No Minna.

Is this what it feels like to be free of obligation? Without ballast? No one to call at five o'clock. No one who cares about the new curtains.

I keep falling. Once when I came out of a dark theater and missed a step. The next time when I slid on water that had spilled from Byron's bowl and needed eleven stitches in my hand. Again in Mexico when I stumbled off a curb and pitched forward into the path of a bus that stopped just in time. And again when my class was coming to the house for an end-of-semester party and I was setting out food. Nothing caused that one to happen. My ankle turned all by itself, breaking a bone in my foot.

Four falls in all, within as many months. Had the ground really been pulled out from under my feet?

I try conducting another experiment with that tree limb out in back of my house. I sit on it for a while, waiting to see if anything will happen. As before, I go on reading a book, but this time the limb doesn't move. She refuses to pass through and go away.

Several months later, I run into Dr. Fisher and ask him something that has been on my mind.

'To a pain specialist, what would the phrase, "the pain of the human condition" mean?'

'Strictly speaking, it doesn't mean a thing, at least not neurologically.'

I wouldn't want to be a neurologist if knowing the body's circuitry kept me from apprehending a deeper truth: that the pain of the human condition is death, the one condition we never get over. And it means we all lose parts of ourselves along the way. No one survives intact. No one is exempt. In that democracy of sorrow lies our consolation.

'Together we've lost about three and a half pounds since we first met.' For a moment, my old friend doesn't get it, and responds as to a report on successful dieting. 'No,' I say, patting my flat left chest and looking significantly at hers, just as flat and far more recently.

JoAnn is looking beautiful. I'd been a bit nervous about seeing her; we're in touch by phone, but I don't get to be with her all that often. I knew about her recently shaved head, a gesture of one-upping the inevitable, but I didn't know what she'd look like. On one coast-to-coast call, she told me about her first venture out as a bald woman, to her local SoHo cafe, where she's a regular. The young crew-cutted waitress who floated around in a peignoir and Doc Martens, and had never paid any attention to JoAnn, began treating her as though she were suddenly cool, an interesting person after all.

JoAnn and I order coffee. I haul a shopping bag onto the cafe table and begin laying out scarves, flipping through them like pages of a well-thumbed book. The top one I'd recently laundered, a soft Egyptian cotton, blush pink with an ivory border. I'd ironed it especially to show how much more attractive the rest of the scarves will eventually look, wrinkled now from having been in my drawer for years.

I call them the K.W. Headcovering Collection, in fond remembrance of my friends springing into action when I learned I had to have chemotherapy, delivering Kate and her no longer needed scarves to my door. To JoAnn I now show a black, white, and yellow silk scarf with the initials YSL. A handblocked scarf from India, burnt orange entwined with magenta, dotted with tiny mirrors. A navy-and-white-striped cotton square, quite smart, quite French. I should have returned these scarves years ago, but instead I'm passing them on to JoAnn.

We disappear into the ladies room and show each other our scars, which are more or less the same, allowing for her still-inflamed redness and the slightly more hollow dent of mine. I show her a ravishing new bra of which I am so proud, with its black lace that lets both the real and the prosthetic breast peep through. With the prosthesis slipped into its pocket like a visiting card into a glove, no one would guess I'm faking it.

It's time to leave. I'm meeting Steve uptown at a show at the Guggenheim. JoAnn and I stand outside the plate-glass window of the cafe. I find myself reaching over to pat her cheek, a gesture that reminds me of something my grandmother might have done. Then I'm seized with love for her.

In the great spiral hall of the museum, I stand for a long time looking at a piece by the German artist Rebecca Horn. She has strung a wire from ceiling to floor. Along its length, a beat-up brown suitcase ascends and descends, slowly opening and shutting, like palms needing to touch.

Minna's mistrust has been eating away at me. Should I write her about how upset and hurt I was?

When I was weeding out my Mother files, I found the contract from the funeral home, specifying a graveside funeral and signed by my mother.

I sent it with a terse little note: 'Just to let you know, this is what my mother did want.'

I wish I could have given my dad's old chair to my father-in-law, but I can't remember where it went. The arms of his own chair are set too far back from the edge of the seat. As he slides himself forward, he has to reach way behind the rest of his body. When he rises, he keeps holding on so that his arms end up pushing his upper body forward until his torso is parallel with the floor. As he tries to straighten, he teeters dangerously. I'd teeter too.

I don't know whether we can find the right chair in Steve's small Wisconsin hometown; it has to be one that tilts so far forward it brings Doc almost to a standing position. But we hit the jackpot: the perfect chair, a color that will fit into the living room and all the features anyone could want, including a rakish setting for 'massage.'

The chair must be brought into the house surreptitiously because Doc might veto the plan if he knew about it. He's leery of large expenditures, not because he's tight but because his needs have always been simple. He tends to be content with what he has. He says he keeps going each day by finding one thing that makes him happy. 'It's doesn't have to be a big thing, but as long as I can find it, I'm all right.'

The doorbell rings. Doc looks up questioningly. A large man is standing in the doorway with a chair in his arms.

'Where do you want this?'

Doc's first thought is Waste Not.

'What are you going to do about this chair?' he asks Steve, tapping his index finger on the faded brocaded armrest. 'It's still a good chair.'

Steve assures him we'll find another place for it.

'How much did this thing cost you?'

'You don't have to know; it's a present, Dad.'

The delivery man places the new chair beside the old one so we can easily slide one away and put the other in its place.

It's time for dinner. Doc struggles to his feet in the usual way. Steve plops down in the new chair and demonstrates what it can do.

His father leans on his walker looking skeptical.

'You try it, Dad.'

It takes both of us to turn him around and back him into the chair. He sits with the remote control in his hand.

'What am I supposed to do with this gizmo?'

'Just press it – no, here – '

The chair lifts, rises, and tilts, depositing him on his feet, his hands free to grasp the walker in front of him.

As Doc walks arduously into the dinette, he can manage only the beginning of a sentence.

'To tell you the truth – '

I hold my breath.

A kitchen chair is scraped back.

Will Doc grant Steve the pleasure I've known, of being able to provide? When he has to acknowledge needing his son's help?

' – I've always wanted a chair like that,' Doc says in a frail but satisfied voice.

'There really isn't any question. It's your own family; you'll have to go back sometime.' So says a friend, and she's right.

Minna will be ninety-three soon. She has become so tiny that her doctor forbids her to go out; in a high wind she could be blown away. I may not have another chance for a visit, just the two of us.

'Why did you send me that funeral contract? I don't understand.'

'Because you questioned my choice. You said I should have had the funeral in the chapel.'

'Did I say that? I can't believe it . . .'

'Steve was with me, so he can tell you it's true. If it had been up to me, of course I would have had it in the chapel; I didn't want to be cold any more than you did. But this is something I did in deference to my mother's wishes. She was very firm about it.'

'I'm sorry, I wouldn't hurt you for the world; you know that, don't you? I must have been out of my mind. When someone dies, people go crazy for a while. I've been so worried. I thought maybe I'd lost you. I couldn't stand that.'

Later over coffee, I ask, 'How did you stay whole, Minna, when so many people around you were falling apart?'

'Sometimes I wonder if I did.'

'Minna!'

'I think what saved me is that I had a sense of possibility. You remember, I always used to say to you, "You never can tell what's around the corner." And when I was little, books saved me. They were my escape in that crazy house. *Heidi* was my favorite. Can you imagine – I used to envy a little girl in a storybook because she lived in a house that was calm?

'I read the newspaper every day from cover to cover, and I think things through differently. Maybe I'm getting a little smarter in my old age. I make it into a challenge to think of something beyond myself.'

Doc says, 'Find one thing that makes you happy.'

Minna says, 'Think of something beyond yourself.'

If I put 'No one survives intact' into my eyeglass case, and then put these other two over it, there'll be a surplus of wisdom inside the case.

The phone rings: Ellie, checking to make sure everything's all right. It was inevitable that we talk. I've schooled myself to act as though nothing has happened, but I'm stilted, and we speak in the language we have in common.

'I'm glad you're there. I feel better knowing someone's in the house with her.'

She can't resist adding a cautionary note.

'Don't tire her out.'

'So often I wonder if things could have turned out differently. Could I have been a writer? I don't know; it's all so long ago. But I know I had deep ecstatic feelings inside me. And in my own way, I tried. What might Herbie have become if he hadn't been so sick – look at how all along he was taking everything into that poor brain of his. Who knows what any of us might have become?

'Sometimes it all feels like it's a hundred thousand years ago. But then other times it's like yesterday. I'll wake up and feel guilty because I haven't called Francie. I talk about it with my therapist.'

'What therapist?'

'I heard about him when your mother was in the Home. I'm probably foolish, a woman my age. At this stage in life I'm not going to change. But I see things differently. You know he comes to the house, which he doesn't have to do. I used to offer him cookies and cake, but he didn't want them. He comes at the end of his day and he looks tired, so now I ask him if he wants some cranberry juice. "That would be lovely," he says, and I feel better already.'

'You're amazing. Sometimes I think I was born with three muses standing by my cradle: your wisdom, my mother's love of beauty, my dad's gusto. Although Francie and Herbie were probably there too.'

'Don't forget. Your mother was the brave one.'

When Ellie and I talked about what happened between us, she said, 'It must have been grief.' There should be a moratorium on hard feelings after a death. Nobody knows what they're saying, everyone's crazy, and forgiveness takes too long.

The next day I drive out to Nantasket, where my father used to drive an ice-cream truck before I was born. Ellie remembers hearing its three-note chime and hot-footing it over the sand for the free cone he'd always give her.

When I was growing up, we spent every summer here, renting a room with kitchen privileges at Mrs. DeVito's on the bay, or Ida Cohen's on A Street near the beach, where my friends and I cooked wieners over a fire. We sat in a circle, my father singing 'On Top of Old Smokey,' then gesturing for us to sing along: *All covered in snow* . . .

At the far end of Nantasket, a narrow causeway connects the town to Hull, an old colonial town whose historic houses bear plaques with dates of origin. A small library, its gray clapboard looking freshly painted, stands in the center of town.

I tell the librarian I used to come here as a child, that it was a place of pilgrimage. I ask whether the library has any of my books. She enters a title in the now-computerized files; sure enough, my name comes up. I'm so pleased.

I look up the call letters for Auden's *Selected Poetry* and find the elegy for Yeats that had stirred me so. Reading it now, its lines seem to be etched in my palm.

Herbie had been there all along:

> Silence invaded the suburbs,
> The current of his feeling failed

Mrs. Landsman's fate was there:

> In the nightmare of the dark
> All the dogs of Europe bark.

And I was part of the poem too:

> For poetry . . . survives, . . .
> A way of happening, a mouth.

I wish I could tell my parents that something in me has changed. I had said there's only a chaotic and impersonal force in the universe. But when I found myself crying, 'What did I do wrong?' I joined an ancient line of human beings calling out for answers.

I went looking for explanations. I had anticipated a world of cause and effect, much as it was pictured on my father's coffee mug. Instead, I've found out how much is uncertain.

I had wanted a world in which everything could be made 'good as new,' or better. I placed my faith in what Dr. MacKenzie called 'human engineering,' to which I added the pressure of human will. Instead, I've seen how much cannot be fixed.

I had wanted to rest in knowledge. Instead, I've learned that our minds are constantly remaking themselves. I had wanted to pin down memory, find a location for it in my brain. Instead, I've learned that memory is diasporic.

I had wanted to track down a single origin for damage. Instead, I've learned there's a location in the brain for bringing many parts together: the frontal lobes. Against their destruction, I set my words.

'I have to tell you one last story about Francie,' Minna says. 'When she was dying, Harry was a patient in the hospital too, one floor below her. Francie hadn't seen him in all those years. When I told her – I had to – she said to me, "I won't be here anymore," and asked to be wheeled down to say goodbye to him.

'She didn't go in. She just sat in the doorway. The two of them looked at each other for a few minutes without saying anything. Then Francie said, "All right, Harry. That's it."

'I took her back upstairs. I told her, "I'm so proud of you, Francie. That took real strength." At the end, she showed what she still had in her.

'For years, Harry was the bad one. Our whole family hated him for what he did to her. But we did plenty of damage too. I should have stood up to Jen, but I didn't. It was wrong.'

There's nothing I can say to that.

'You saw things a child never should have seen, Herbie, Francie . . .'

'It's true, Minna. But I'm not damaged by them.'

'Please forgive us.'

'Minna, sometimes we can choose what we want to remember. Here's what I choose. Do you know my father used to visit Harry at the Home, even though Harry was so far gone by then he couldn't recognize anyone?

'My dad would bring a pair of scissors with him so that he could trim Harry's hair. I used to be amazed that he'd go on taking care of Harry after everything that had happened.

'When I asked him why he did it, my father said with a characteristic shrug, as though it were obvious, "Someone's got to – look, he's a human being, isn't he?" '

Phantom limb begins with dis-membering, but it can become re-membering. My father left me an inheritance after all. I think of Miss G., who had seemed so pathetic years ago. How she cherished her ring; not the jewel but the presence of the person who had given it to her. Of no value, it had kept significance. I think that's what we all want to keep in the end.

The movers are due to arrive early in the morning. I race to an ATM machine to get cash for tips, barely making it back when the doorbell rings and two young men are standing there, one looking as if he should be in the cast of a musical about bohemian youth, the other like a Czech tennis champion.

'Where do you want this?'

'I don't know yet; could you move it into this room just this once; I need to see how it looks . . . nope, sorry, could you move it back?'

They're accommodating, and besides it turns out, after all, there's less than I'd remembered – a table, a wing chair, the rose velvet sofa. Smaller things we put on the kitchen table – his cribbage set; a statuette of a brass boy saluting, given to him by the Cub Scouts. Her cake plates. My old books, King of the Wind, Famous Paintings for Young People, The Door in the Wall.

For now, paintings are stacked against a wall, Dorothy's laundry on a clothesline, slated for the guest bedroom, that portrait of me as a chubby little girl smiling serenely.

Is that really me? What's so awful about it anyway?

Then it hits. There's no more discussion of the merits of the painting. There's no more furniture coming. No more questions, no more lists. These things – this is what remains. This is it.

The movers have gone, leaving me to look around at what's here. Once, I'd placed the inconsolability of loss against the visible signs of consolation. Now I see the rooms, the objects, the words as consolatory once more. Memories may be diasporic, but they can also be congregant, telling me I'm not alone.

This afternoon, the old heavy artificial leg will be leaving, picked up by a nearby rehab center that will adapt it for someone else to use. This is the last time I can look at it, the time when I must not turn away.

I sit in front of it, cross-legged. With the rolls of gift wrapping paper still inside, the leg is a head taller than I am. The toes are slightly darker than the rest of the foot, as though the leg has been out in the sun. The foot ends a little below the ankle where a solid piece of wood, shaped like a funnel and painted a soft pink, rises to the beginning of the calf. At that point the leg becomes a brace of brown leather, the color of a fine saddle.

Handsome brown laces are threaded through brass eyelets in the back. Metal rods rise vertically the entire length of the leg. At the top rim an ivory leather strap connects to a waist belt. More straps keep the upper leg in place, adjustable by pulling on dangling metal rings. For about three inches between the upper and lower parts of the prosthesis, space has been left empty between the rods in order to accommodate the real knee.

I put my arm inside the leg as far as it can go, as though it were a sleeve. I wave the leg in the air, like someone saying goodbye to a departing ship.

With my arm still inside the leg, I bend at the elbow and place the leg on my lap. I lay the foot in the crook of my other elbow. I'm cradling her limb in my arms.

I've remained fascinated by Madame I. After the report was published, her case was no longer followed. Denys and Camus ended their account with these words: 'She claims that she is lost, that her disease is incurable; she accepts neither treatment nor consolation.'

The researchers did not solve the mystery of Madame I's compulsion to rub herself 'as though trying to confirm that her body existed.' Perhaps Madame I had discovered, all on her own, the instructions of the visiting nurse: for my mother, to generate a phantom limb; for Madame I, to bring forth another phantom, a continuous memory.

It is 1907, a good year to be in Paris. Atget lugs his camera everywhere. Proust observes his friends. Madame I is walking in the Bois, greeting acquaintances.

She strolls past my mother, the two women exchanging a nod of recognition when, with no warning, Madame I drops to the pavement with a sharp cry. She is helped to her feet by passers-by, my mother among them. Along with all else that has been restored to her, Madame I now can feel pain.

Once recovered, did Madame I ever long for her painless days? She's talking this over with my mother in the garden behind her house. They are sitting at an iron table, on ground covered with pebbles. On the table are violets; in the far distance, the clamor of children at play.

My mother asks Madame I whether she thinks remembering is worth it, if it brings pain.

Madame I answers tartly: 'That's nonsense. Do you realize what I'd lost? I couldn't imagine the taste of food, nor the scent of flowers. I'd forgotten my parents, even how my own children sound.'

From across the garden, voices draw nearer. 'I can hear my children,' says Madame I. 'At last.'

ACKNOWLEDGMENTS

I am fortunate in having friends skilled in critique, wise in understanding, and generous of spirit. For their willingness to read several drafts of this book, I owe special thanks to Irene Borger, JoAnn Callis, Bette Korman, James Lapine, and Paul Zelevansky.

This book has also benefited from the enthusiastic support and sensitive responses of Barbara Abrash, Perry Miller Adato, Loretta Barrett, James Bono, Karen Braziller, Tony Cohan, Margit Cotsen, Peggy Daniel, Herman Engel, Saul Friedlander, Sonya Friedman, Elyse and Stanley Grinstein, Ana Maria Gutierrez, Patricia Hampl, Linda Huggins, Gabrielle Idlet, Mary Jansen, Joy Johannessen, Elaine Koss, Hillel Levine, Randi Markowitz, members of the Women's Lunch Group, Deena Metzger, Richard Metzner, Diane Middlebrook, Honor Moore, Joseph Olshan, Alan Rachins, Hilda Raz, Lynn Rosenfeld, Jane St. Clair, Karen Sacks, Peter Sacks, Joseph Somerset, and Sherry Sonnett, especially for her words, "Resilience is demanded of us again and again." Thank you. You are all part of this book.

Special thanks are due my learned and benevolent guide to neurology, Dr. Lawrence Kruger, Professor Emeritus of Neurobiology and Anesthesiology at the University of California, Los Angeles. Of the many useful books about cognitive science, I especially want to acknowledge the book that introduced me to Madame I, *The Strange, Familiar and Forgotten*, by Israel Rosenfield.

This book includes revised or altered versions of the following previously published material: "Journal from a Semi-Private Room," *Conditions*, no. 4 (1979): 14-29; "The Scan Chronicles" in *Living on the Margins: Women Writers on Breast Cancer*, ed. Hilda Raz (Persea: New York, 1999), 260-73; "Without the Wig," *Culturefront* 8, no. 1 (1999): 63-64; "Trochaic," *Prairie Schooner* 71, no. 1 (1997): 230-33; and "His Regular Fare," *Prairie Schooner* 71, no. 1 (1997): 234.

To my parents, Helen and Samuel B. Sternburg, and my aunt, Etta Somerset, this book owes its existence and heart. While based on fact, several of the people in this book became composite characters as the manuscript took shape. I thank my relatives for understanding this process.

Finally, and first in dedication: to my husband, Steven D. Lavine, for your wholehearted giving of all that is best, your brilliance, kindness, and love. At the center of my life is the love I offer, now and always, to you.

Janet Sternburg was born and raised in Boston, Massachusetts. She is the author and editor of both volumes of *The Writer on Her Work*, the classic collections on what it means to be a woman who writes. A widely published poet and essayist, she is also a photographer whose work is in private and museum collections. As former director of Writers in Performance, she is known for creating new ways to present literature on stage. Married to Steven Lavine, she resides in New York and teaches at the California Institute of the Arts.